Language and Politics in
Julia Kristeva

SUNY series in Psychoanalysis and Culture
Henry Sussman, editor

Language and Politics in Julia Kristeva

Literature, Art, Therapy

Carol Mastrangelo Bové

Marianne Surgent
fendes, été 2006

State University of New York Press

Published by
State University of New York Press, Albany

For information, address State University of New York Press,
194 Washington Avenue, Suite 305, Albany, NY 12210-2384

Production by Marilyn P. Semerad
Marketing by Anne M. Valentine

Library of Congress Cataloging-in-Publication Data

Bové, Carol Mastrangelo.
    Language and politics in Julia Kristeva : literature, art, therapy / Carol
Mastrangelo Bové.
        p. cm.—(SUNY series in psychoanalysis and culture)
    Includes bibliographical references and index.
    ISBN 0-7914-6649-3 (hardcover : alk. paper)—ISBN 0-7914-6650-7 (pbk :
    alk. paper)
    1. Kristeva, Julia, 1941—Criticism and interpretation.   I. Title.   II. Series.

PN75.K75B68 2005
801'.95'092—dc22   2005004416

ISBN-13: 978-0-7914-6649-0 (hardcover : alk. paper)
ISBN-13: 978-0-7914-6650-6 (pbk : alk. paper)

                    10 9 8 7 6 5 4 3 2 1

For Daniel O'Hara, in friendship.

❦ Contents ❧

❧ Acknowledgments ❧

I thank Julia Kristeva for the work that inspired my book, for reading the manuscript, and for permission to use her website picture on the cover. I want to express my appreciation to Paul Bové for his many helpful comments throughout the time I worked on this project. Daniel O'Hara and Marcia Landy read the manuscript and offered useful suggestions for which I am grateful. As always, Serge Doubrovsky, Gerald Prince, and Marilyn Rose supported me in this project. I also want to thank Westminster College for providing me with sabbatical time to complete it, Joseph and Elizabeth Henderson for the Lectureship Award that supported me in the early stages of the manuscript, Ann Murphy for the scheduling that facilitated the work, and Ellen Venema and Jennifer Corkadel for help in preparing the manuscript. Friends, and in particular, Phyllis Ktzerow and Bethany Hicok, showed an interest in my writing that sustained me especially as I completed it. Finally, Laura Bové inspired me with her energy and critical spirit to get the job done.

Four of the chapters in this book were previously published in different form and with different titles as journal essays. Grateful acknowledgment is made to the editors and publishers of these journals.

"The Politics of Desire in Julia Kristeva." *boundary 2*, 12 (1984): 217–28.

"Women and Society in Literature, or Reading Kristeva and Proust." "After Theory," *Dalhousie Review* 64, no. 2 (1984): 260–69.

"The Twin Faces of the Mother's Mask: Julia Kristeva's *Powers of Horror: An Essay on Abjection.*" *Discourse* 11, no. 1 (1988–89): 151–56.

"Revisiting Modernism with Kristeva: DeBeauvoir, Truffaut, and Renoir." *Journal of Modern Literature* 25, 3–4 (2002): 114–26.

❧ Introduction ❧

For more than three decades, a variety of writers throughout the world have increasingly made reference to Julia Kristeva's work. Her psychoanalytic writing narrates the life and work of individuals and their creative coping with personal and public forms of domination. With a focus on the psyche as expressed in language, she examines psychic formations and how they shape, and are in turn shaped by, social hierarchies.

Her political intervention is that of the intellectual. Concrete and public like the activist's work, she writes in an effort to elicit dialogue and encourage action. She has also intervened more directly in social events, organizing discussion groups in the aftermath of May '68 and speaking publicly in 1999 in favor of the French parity law by recognizing the social meaning of reproduction and the need for mothers to be represented on the ballot.

This book analyzes the politics, that is, the principles relating to power and status, embodied in her theory and fiction from 1969 to 2004, which in various ways tell the stories of creative individuals and their psychic dilemmas. Through these individuals, Kristeva identifies significant psychic structures and their impact on social stratification. Her work over the past thirty years or so, like that of Hélène Cixous and of Luce Irigaray with whom her name is often linked, raises questions about the nature, strengths, and limits of psychoanalytic writing. Her theory and fiction succeed in describing psychic formations that transcend the individual and develop out of particular gender associations. Does such writing sufficiently attend

1

to historical conditions as well as to class and race? How does one use the categories "masculine" and "feminine" without gender bias, that is, without fixing gender identity in overly rigid definitions or "essences," for example, that "the feminine" is masochistic?

Psychoanalytic theory has been an influential part of critical debate in the humanities and social sciences for many years particularly since May '68 in Paris. This theory has, for example, had considerable impact on feminist and film studies and continues to do so as I show in chapters 3 and 4. An examination of the often intense debate, particularly on the problem of essentialism, provides a greater understanding of three decades of theory emerging in the French capital. With roots in Sigmund Freud's groundbreaking work, psychoanalytic theorists including Kristeva, Jacques Lacan, Hélène Cixous, and Luce Irigaray employ the categories "male/female" in analyzing psychic formations and social hierarchies. My examination of Kristeva's work necessarily becomes engaged in continuing critical debates over the strengths and limits of psychoanalytic writing and the questions it poses (see, for instance, Jacqueline Rose, Toril Moi, Kelly Oliver, Gayatri Spivak, Nancy Fraser, and Druscilla Cornell). This book demonstrates that in Kristeva's psychoanalytic writing it is possible both to describe "male" and "female" across time and place and to identify the historical conditions differentiating individual lives. For Kristeva, as for Cixous and Irigaray, language is gender-inflected and has an impact on the distribution of power between the sexes and among other groups often associated with "the female," for example, "the Jew." My study acknowledges that both categories are problematic and liable to essentializing (see pp. 6, 88).

The book also confirms certain limits that such critics as Spivak have helped to identify in psychoanalytic theory including Kristeva's. While her writing overall shows an awareness of conditions shaped by history, race, and class, there are times when she neglects to analyze these conditions in sufficient detail. Furthermore, her understanding of the "feminine" and "masculine" come dangerously close to essentializing. The "feminine" in particular appears to identify the woman as masochistic and to deny the ways in which Western societies construct sexuality and gender.

This book shows how Kristeva's theory makes possible innovative interpretations of both canonical and little-known writers and directors some of whom have not been read in the context of her work, including Marcel Proust, Simone De Beauvoir, Jean Renoir, and François Truffaut. An outline of the arguments and strategies of Kristeva's books in mostly chronological order uncovers her principal insights into psychic formations in the West and their role in shaping power relationships. While I sometimes refer to the French versions of her work (parts of which are not available in English), I give special emphasis to the large portion of her writing that is translated and therefore accessible to a broader audience. This work includes many of the texts that have been most influential in the United States and England, the fifteen volumes published by Columbia University Press and *About Chinese Women* (*Des Chinoises*, 1974, Marion Boyars).

Like many European critics of the twentieth century for whom Marx as well as Freud has been an undeniable influence—Walter Benjamin is one example—Kristeva frequently draws a parallel between language, on the one hand, and social stratification, on the other. Unlike Marx for whom such stratification, "class struggle" in his terms, is fundamental and gives rise to "intellectual production" and "consciousness" (*The Communist Manifesto*), for Kristeva, it is primarily the other way around: language and the psychic structures embodied in it influence and produce social hierarchies or the political. In this book I argue that Kristeva's abiding project in these years and today is to theorize the kind of language that creates a degree of control over one's life and, in the broadest sense, confronts and helps transform repressive political structures.

The first chapter studies *Revolution in Poetic Language* (*La Révolution du langage poétique*, 1974) as a starting point in Kristeva's theory. This volume erects a psychoanalytic theory of art and a critique of Western capitalism that continues throughout her work. For Kristeva, capitalism organizes the circulation of people for their exchange value; it is a political and economic system emerging out of a psychic formation repressing the many ways individuals speak and become transformed in language. Thus, a capitalist society represses signifying practice understood as a process of becoming. Focusing on Lautréamont and Mallarmé, *Revolution in Poetic Language* is part and parcel of Kristeva's overall project through her book *Colette*: to theorize the signifying practice, especially in literary creation, that gives shape to the material and rational process of becoming. For Kristeva, "material" derives from the Freudian notion of the mother as a physical and imaginary base for the psyche; the "rational" may be understood in terms of the "social and historical content" of symbolic language, as in Hegel's "thetic position." From a Kristevan perspective, "signifying practice," a process that transforms the psyche, constitutes a deconstruction of the unified self and the rebirth of a rational position enabling the reconstruction of changed social relations.

Revolution is a clear example of the way Kristeva attempts both to describe the psychic formations transcending individuals in Mallarmé's poems and to pay attention to historical conditions, the discontent of the working class in 1848–71. She has been charged with an inadequate attention to history, for example, in her analysis of Chinese women, *About Chinese Women*. While the charge is undeserved in this volume and overall, in *Revolution* one would like a fuller explanation of the historical context and content of Mallarmé's poems. Despite the overly brief discussion of his references to the working class, Kristeva's analysis of Mallarmé reveals the role of conflict in the sexual and familial dynamics that generate social relations and that periodically bring about change in their structure.

In Kristeva's theory, as introduced in *Revolution* in chapter 1, the writer uses language in order to give shape to the unconscious drives that constitute subjectivity. She builds on Lacan's reading of Freud and in particular on the notion of a multiple speaking subject whose "unconscious is structured as a language." Kristeva's theory, however, shifts the emphasis from Freud's and Lacan's concepts of the father and the phallus to that of sexual difference. Kristeva's 1980 *Desire in Language* (the volume I discuss in some detail in chapter 2), includes essays on a wide range of French, Russian, and Irish writers including DeLaSale, Mayakovsky, Khlebnikov, Céline, Beckett, Sollers, Barthes, and Bakhtin. Considered as a whole, these essays demonstrate that, in light of the Kristevan notion of the subject, earlier critical concepts of author and aesthetic unity are inadequate and are based on a tradition of rational discourse. I distinguish Kristeva's theory from that of other psychoanalytic theorists including, for example, Jeffrey Mehlman, for whom discourse is understood as a form of sublimation and evidence of the normal resolution of the Oedipal conflict. In these theorists, sublimation produces cultural order and, in political terms, reinforces the status quo. While Kristeva recognizes the need for a degree of unity in the text in order to communicate, she emphasizes the way in which the text at times breaks with communicative language and with the social contract.

Chapters 2 and 3 use Kristeva's work to help read a specific text, Marcel Proust's *Remembrance of Things Past*. In light of her theory, *Remembrance* constitutes an implicit criticism of one model of the French Symbolist movement and, more generally, of the unified male authority figure underlying patriarchal structures, including this movement, the salon, and capitalist society in general. While I make reference to Kristeva's reading of Proust in her later *Time and Sense*, I use my reading of Proust as the point of departure to examine in some detail the ways in which Kristeva's psychoanalytic theory is critical of patriarchy and can be considered feminist despite her rejection of that label.

Kristeva's work is instrumental in reinterpreting patriarchal structures in other classic novels and films including Simone DeBeauvoir's *She Came to Stay*, François Truffaut's *Jules and Jim*, and Jean Renoir's *Rules of the Game*. Taking these works as examples, chapter 4 examines the conflicts monogamy imposes on a heroine struggling for a degree of independence in her physical and psychic life. I show that Kristeva's theory makes clear the significance of the heroine's struggle as an individual within the sexual/political relationships that reproduce this struggle on a social level. The female protagonist's effort, part of a politics that is socially and sexually radical, is also that of Modernism, or as Kristeva calls it "Modernité," the artistic movement emerging in Europe at roughly the same time as psychoanalysis and feminism. In this chapter particularly and throughout my book, reference to the many writers relevant to a discussion of her theory as it informs a rereading of canonical texts—and especially of the Modernist canon—provides some of the critical context for Kristeva's thought. They include Mikhail Bakhtin, André Bazin, Maurice Merleau-Ponty, Paul Ricoeur, and Jacqueline Rose. This chapter and its wide range of reference demonstrate the interdisciplinary nature of Kristeva's work by revealing the implications of her theory for not only literature but also film and philosophy. Her recent trilogy on *Feminine Genius,* including volumes on the philosopher Hannah Arendt, the psychoanalyst Melanie Klein, and the novelist Colette, further reveals how her work transcends disciplinary limits and, more important, moves away from the study of figures of the male—and not just from male authors—to those of sexual difference as I explain.

Chapter 5 contributes to the debate on the most troubling components of Kristeva's politics: her writing on Céline and on Maoist China (in *Powers of Horror: An Essay on Abjection* [*Povvoirs de l'horreur: Essai sur l'abjection,* 1981], *About Chinese Women* [*Des Chinoises,* 1974], and *The Samurai* [*Les Samurai's,* 1990]). *Powers of Horror,* for example, is among the most controversial of Kristeva's theoretical texts because of the association of the abject with "the woman" and "the Jew." Kristeva uses the term "abjection" to refer to the simultaneous attraction and repulsion for the body that derives from the moment when the child's symbiosis with the mother is interrupted. *Powers of Horror* uncovers abjection in Judeo-Christian religious practices such as Judaism's elaborate purification rites. This volume also shows how Louis-Ferdinand Céline creates scenarios in which confrontations with the body in the form of women and Jews provoke psychic crises in a subject imprisoned within French rationalism and the social hierarchies with which it is linked, as I describe in this chapter. Kristeva's concept of abjection exemplifies the problem of essentialism raised by psychoanalytic theory: her association of "the woman" and "the Jew" with the abject may appear both sexist and racist. A reading of her book and of the historical documentation provided reveals that, according to Kristeva, Céline's fiction depicts a subject caught within the sexist and anti-Semitic stratification of early twentieth-century French life and thought. For Kristeva, Céline is a novelist who presents alternatives to contemporary hierarchies (though as a writer of political pamphlets, he unfortunately does not). I show how Kristeva herself supports the alternatives in her own writing strategies.

In *Tales of Love* (*Histoires d'amour*, 1983), *In the Beginning Was Love* (*Au Commencement était l'amour: Psychanalyse et foi*, 1985), and *Black Sun* (*Soleil noir: Dépression et mélancholie*, 1987), Kristeva brings her psychoanalytic method to bear on art, religion, and everyday experience. I consider Kristeva's belief that writing has an impact on the distribution of power in the discussion of these books in chapter 6 by examining both what she says on this subject and what she implies in the form of her writing. One of the implications of *Tales of Love* is that the writer, for example, the seventeenth-century mystic Jeanne Guyon, achieves a partial autonomy in writing vis-à-vis threatening familial and religious hierarchies (in a form different from the usual union of male mystic with male God in Western mysticism discussed by Jeffrey Kripal). In "Stabat Mater," the best-known chapter in this volume, Kristeva gives a psychoanalytic reading of childbirth, a topic that in her view is frequently repressed. Her reading of childbirth goes deeper than lifting the repression from a topic for discussion: she demonstrates how giving birth constitutes a rejection of a masochistic or abject mother as the first stage prior to living within a social contract. The chapter is an instance—more fully developed than in *Powers of Horror*—of the ways in which her work appears to fix gender identity in stereotype. She describes the woman as representative of Western culture repudiating the mother in order to exist. My reading of "Stabat Mater" reveals that, prior to repudiation, the woman recreates the early symbiosis with the mother within language. Thus, rejecting the abject mother is not ultimately essentialist but is part of a dual moment that goes on indefinitely as the subject constructs and deconstructs its fragile identity.

Following Freud, in *Black Sun*, Kristeva employs the concept of an androgynous figure, the imaginary or loving father, not unlike Freud's father of individual prehistory in *Group Psychology*. She studies both the Dutch painter Hollbein and Ann, one of her patients, showing how they are both initially caught in a depressive state in which they refuse to separate from a dead mother, dominated by depression and their enslavement to a maternal figure. Each eventually proceeds to a vital identification with a loving father.

The seventh chapter reveals that Kristeva's more recent work, her last two novels, *The Old Man and the Wolves* (*Le vieil homme et les loups*, 1994) and *Possessions* (*Possessions*, 1996) and the last volume of her trilogy on female intellectuals *Colette* (*Colette*, 2002), is among her most compelling. I show that a number of elements in Kristeva's theory, as introduced in *Revolution in Poetic Language*, also shape her novels, literary embodiments of her theory yet not dependent on it. Like her theory, Kristeva's novels tell the story of threatening psychic confrontations with pain and death as her characters identify with maternal and paternal figures. The protagonists' quest for pleasure, the reversals in the roles of child and parent, and the political/ethical commitment to helping others both directly and in her writing are other components of both Kristeva's theory and fiction, as I will show.

I also demonstrate how tragic consequences compel an awareness of the unconscious and of its psychic identifications in her theory, later novels, and study of Colette. My hypothesis in this chapter is that Kristeva's fiction and her examination of Colette's life and work are as compelling as her theory when the element of masochism, which does not function primarily as female stereotype in her work, is more prominent in the psyches she describes.

In evaluating her contributions in the final chapter of the book, I return to two perceived weaknesses in her writing discussed earlier (chapters 1, 5, 6, and 7, for example): an inadequate treatment of historical conditions and a masochistic/abject component in her use of the category "woman." While there are places in her theory that require a more thorough discussion of historical particulars, the book concludes that Kristeva's attention to history is more than adequate overall. I also conclude that, while parts of Kristeva's theory and fiction, especially dealing with the abject, contain a masochistic component in that they stress pain, violence, and the death drive, these parts are also the most profound and moving. The use of the abject may enable her more fully to expose and to try to cope with contemporary psychological dangers, steering clear of a utopian vision, as Jacqueline Rose has pointed out.

My book emphasizes the ways in which Kristeva reinvents the concept of author to show how many canonical texts take on new meaning in light of her work, revealing psychological conflicts that mirror those in the family, and in more public institutions such as schools and the state. The Bible, *Voyage to the End of the Night*, and *Remembrance of Things Past* are three significant examples of the way her theory enables a rereading of compelling psychic dramas and their political implications for the twenty-first century. Her writing also reconstitutes the canon periodically by opening it up to marginal figures such as Bakhtin and DeLaSale, making possible productive readings of little known writers. Focused on the psyche as it exists in language, Kristeva's work strives to make institutions more responsive to the individual's and to society's changing needs. I conclude that, from her student days in Paris to her more recent novels and trilogy on female intellectuals, her writing has been consistently committed to help free the subject from domination by sociopolitical hierarchies.

1

The Eruption of Conflict:
Revolution in Poetic Language

Julia Kristeva's early work, *Revolution in Poetic Language* (1974),[1] elaborates a psychoanalytic theory of art whose goal remains radical and constant through the recent volume, *Colette* (2002): to bring about change in the power structures embedded in social relations. Her writing emphasizes the role of psychic conflict in transforming the dynamics of sexuality and of the family. Kristeva's early work is a starting point in her theory of art as a practice that has, as she states, this "social function."

In *Revolution*, Kristeva takes up her project to elaborate an art or "signifying practice" that uncovers the material, rational process of becoming—in other words, the ways in which one speaks in language and in social practice in general. For her, art constitutes a potentially liberating deconstruction of the unified self, the rebirth of a rational position, and changed social relations.

At the same time, Kristeva's rejection of some political theory, coupled with a dialectical methodology, appears to undercut the understanding of art as radical practice in both *Revolution* and her later work including *Tales of Love*. A dialectical methodology creates zones of conflict in her theory and has generated a lively debate over the issues of gender stereotypes (especially the masochistic woman) and essentialist/biologist conceptions of sexual identity. In fact, Kristeva's work has come under attack and elicited controversy over the issue that I see at the heart of her enterprise, the social function of the text. The controversy often takes the form of a discussion of stereotyping or of a minimal attention to history.[2] My hypothesis throughout this book is that her methodology enables Kristeva to confront and to work against the dangers of stereotyping and essentialism.

In *Revolution*, the conflict that splits the subject in the process of living new versions of pre-Oedipal scripts mobilizes her own writing and appears to produce contradictions. In other words, the apparent contradictions in her theory of art's function derive from the conflict in the subject that becomes the driving force behind her dialectical approach. For Kristeva, the subject is conflict-ridden to the point where he or she is no longer a unified self. "Author" and "text" therefore function differently in Kristeva than they do in much of the criticism and theory that has shaped the response to literature over the years.

In *Revolution*, Kristeva analyzes psychic formation or what Kristeva calls "the process of becoming" in the signifying practices of the West. In this section, Kristeva lays out the genealogy of her ideas in detail, connecting her theory to a large number of philosophers, linguists, and psychiatrists including Plato, Hegel, Feuerbach, Marx, Husserl, Benveniste, Frege, Derrida, Lacan, and especially Freud. Both building on their work and distinguishing her own from it, she demonstrates the validity of her thought as a substantial contribution in its own right. With this volume, she lays the foundation for the projects she pursues in the decades to follow.

Kristeva connects art and society from the first page of *Revolution* where she outlines her broad plan: to uncover what Western capitalism represses, the process of becoming underlying signifying practices. For her, to the extent that it privileges the circulation of objects, words, and especially people for their exchange value, capitalism represses signifying practice as a process of becoming and produces isolated disciplines that reify both the "object" of study and the subject caught up in that study. In similar moves to connect art and social structures, she later talks about the "socio-symbolic order" (83) and the "social function" of art (105). She defines this function by saying that the signifying process is uniquely equipped to subvert capitalism by transforming the subject (105).

For Kristeva, art transforms the subject by partially uncovering repressed familial/sexual relationships in formal structures. Revising Freud by giving greater emphasis to sexual difference than to the male figure, she describes how the psyche within the text alternately identifies with an authority figure, the father, and rejects that identification by moving toward the mother. She analyzes, for instance, Mallarmé's deconstruction of the unified self, an entity vital to the capitalist enterprise of late nineteenth-century France. His two poems, *Igitur* and *A Throw of the Dice*, stage a series of conflicting identifications with maternal and paternal figures (211). For Kristeva, these poems reveal the psychic conflicts repressed by upper-middle-class ideology, especially by its concept of a unified self (211). In the years to follow, modern novelists, including James Joyce, as Hélène Cixous demonstrated in *The Exile of James Joyce* (1968), will recreate psychic conflicts and embed them in a rational, social, and historical context, in a "thetic position" to use Kristeva's Hegelian term. Thus, for her, art replays personal conflicts on the more general stage of Western social and cultural history.

In "The Question of Proof in Freud's Psychoanalytic Writings," Paul Ricoeur uses the work of Jürgen Habermas to explore the problematic parallel between political and psychic structures, a parallel that is vital to an understanding of Kristeva's theory.[3] Ricoeur explains that repression in psychoanalysis functions like banishment in the social sciences: repression "banishes a part of language from the public sphere of communication." Psychoanalysis, like the social sciences, is "guided by the interest in emancipation and motivated . . . by the wish to recover the force of Selbstreflexion [self-understanding]." Thus, for Habermas and Ricoeur, as for Kristeva, psychoanalysis reveals the way in which the psyche in the form of writing can have an impact on the distribution of power.

Kristeva develops the terms "symbolic" and "semiotic" (introduced in two essays in her earlier *Semiotica*) at great length in most of the first one hundred pages of *Revolution* to talk with some precision about the formal structures of literature, and more indirectly about its influence on power relations. Briefly put, the symbolic, on the one hand, defines those aspects of a text that communicate by adopting denotation and by following the syntactical rules of language. Here she is borrowing Ferdinand De Saussure's notion of *langue* or linguistic system, as opposed to *parole* or individual speech acts. Symbolic process and *langue* demand an identification with the father as the authority figure representing compliance with the rules of language as part of the social contract.

The semiotic, on the other hand, describes everything in a text that cannot be defined by the symbolic, especially connotations, violations of syntax, and the phonetic resources of language including rhythm. For Kristeva, the semiotic constitutes an identification with the mother as the source of physical pleasure. Semiotic process is prior to symbolic process, yet exists within it. The psyche's discontinuity—in her terms, heterogeneity—derives from the distinction between symbolic and semiotic. Each is linked inextricably to the other while remaining radically different from that other.

Kristeva outlines the history of her conception of the semiotic in Plato's chora, the subject as body movement having a pattern but not yet conceiving itself as unified. Once she sets in motion the interplay of symbolic and semiotic, Kristeva demonstrates the emergence of her theory out of Hegel as well as Plato. She theorizes the movements of symbolic and semiotic in a heterogeneous signifying process using Hegel's dialectical logic and his distinction between "the thetic" and "rejection."

A good example of the process theorized here will appear later in her well-known essay "Stabat Mater" in which she describes the experience of childbirth.[4] She uses the image of her baby as both bone marrow and bone to convey the confusion of self and other in delivery. Childbirth is for her a physical and psychic experience, a contradictory alternation of self and other, of life and death, that is a source and a metaphor for the semiotic and symbolic (see chapter 6).

Kristeva carefully shows the degree to which she builds her theory on such predecessors as Hegel and Plato, acknowledging debts as well as claiming some measure of originality. She derives her notion of the subject's conflicting movements from Hegel, for instance, but points out that she never subsumes them in a synthesizing rational position as he does.

At times, Kristeva seems to contradict her claim that the subject does not ultimately occupy such a position. The distinction she makes between her theory and Hegel's is difficult to see because she frequently states that the semiotic exists within the symbolic and that the symbolic is required for the subject to avoid psychosis. Yet, ultimately, it is the role of the semiotic that she stresses as a fundamental, liberating, and pleasurable moment.[5]

Considered in light of the predecessors who have shaped the response to literature in this century, Kristeva is at a crossroads where formalism, Marxist existentialism, and psychoanalysis intersect. Along with Hegel, two other influential predecessors are the existentialists Jean-Paul Sartre and Simone DeBeauvoir, perhaps the best-known intellectuals of their generation writing in French. Despite their rejection of psychoanalysis, a reading of their fiction, DeBeauvoir's *She Came to Stay* (see chapter 3) and Sartre's *Nausea*, for instance, reveals characters grappling with the very contradictions and conflicts that psychoanalysis delineates so well.

Kristeva's emphasis on discontinuous process in the psyche's movements and in the construction of sexuality along with her critique of the capitalist state's class and gender hierarchies offer striking parallels to existentialism. Toril Moi has noticed some of these parallels in a discussion of the history of feminist theory from DeBeauvoir to Lacan.[6] It is not within the scope of this chapter on *Revolution* to study the relationship between Kristeva and the existentialists in detail. I do, however, want to call attention to certain parallels between Kristeva, on the one hand, and Sartre and DeBeauvoir, on the other, to show more of her theory's context and genealogy.

From a psychoanalytic point of view, these parallels, along with Kristeva's vehement condemnation of existentialism and her preference for Simone Weil over Simone DeBeauvoir, may indicate a degree of anxiety in her own separation from the Mother and/or Father.[7] In *Revolution*, she speaks of Sartre's "full subject, whose economy is never open and never negativized" (212). In *The Samurai*, she sees the engagement of the Sartre-like character Dubreuil (also the name DeBeauvoir uses in *The Mandarins* for the couple resembling herself and Sartre) as ineffective.

The familial relationships that appear to be replayed in Kristeva's critique of the influential DeBeauvoir and Sartre help to situate her work. It emerges in the Paris of the sixties where psychoanalysis and its attack on the self as a capitalist construct mesh with leftist politics, including that of existentialist writers, as Sherry Turkle points out.[8] Kristeva was a student herself at the time, working primarily with Roland Barthes, probably her most immediate influence. His radical semiotic analysis of nineteenth-century realist fiction and of the bourgeois objectification of the psyche and society that informs that fiction also seems to have had a significant impact on her literary theory.[9]

Understood from Kristeva's neo-Freudian perspective and situated this time in turn-of-the-century Paris, the subject's familial relationships play a primary role in Symbolist poetry.[10] In the chapter "Freud's Notion of Expulsion: Rejection," Mallarmé and Lautréamont are the principal examples of her theory that, by uncovering a dynamics hidden in formal structure, literature transforms the subject and society. She outlines how rejection or a movement away from the mother emerges in Mallarmé's *Igitur* and *A Throw of the Dice*. Rejection reveals itself in what Kristeva calls "oralization": the rhythms, preciosity, snobbery, and glottal spasm that suggest the idealized, forbidden mother. In other words, she describes Mallarmé's attempt in these two poems to narrate the birth of the poet as a movement away from the mother that is at the same time a celebration of the pleasures of oral gratification. In a pre-Oedipal stage prior to entry into language, the subject separates from the mother and earlier physical dependency when the mouth sucked at the breast. Oralization, a gestural language, enables the subject/poet both to repeat the earlier experience and to create a new one. He then continues on the path to the symbolic by next identifying with a father figure. This subsequent movement in the poet's narrative occurs when he identifies with Hegel as a patriarchal figure representing the synthesis of the material world within a dialectic that is also rational. To use Kristeva's terms, rejection reappears as "homo-sexual phratry" in Mallarmé's Hegelian philosophy.

Later in her analysis of Mallarmé's two poems, Kristeva discusses the emergence of the dice game and chance that come to replace symbolic function. The dice game takes the form of a transgression against the mother who tries to hide the mysteries of his sexuality from the poet, "The mother is the keeper of the last, the most radical, the most insidious prohibition, the one that safeguards the race's continuity by maintaining the mystery around the process of the subject (which Freud was to unveil by analyzing sexuality and which Mallarmé explores through the language of madness denied)" (229). In this part of Kristeva's analysis, the mother plays the role of authority figure or father, and the poet's disobedience is, in fact, a turning away from that father.

These conflicting movements toward both parents suggest that the subject may be moving not so much toward two different parents as toward the male and female components of a single androgynous parent, as Richard Klein noticed in his article on *Revolution*.[11] An androgynous figure becomes prominent in Kristeva's description of the imaginary Father in her later works, *Tales of Love* and *Black Sun*.

Kristeva connects Mallarmé's project to the discontent of the working classes during the 1848–71 period when the upper-middle-class state, especially Louis Napoleon's empire, accumulated great wealth at their expense. She shows how Mallarmé's poetry uncovers the psychic conflicts repressed by an ideology that exploits human beings on two levels, the psychic and the economic. She writes, "Expending thought through the signifying process, the text inscribes the negativity that (capitalist) society and its official ideology repress. . . . it thus dissents from the dominant economic and ideological system" (*Revolution*, 186). For Kristeva, Mallarmé's texts give life to the psychic struggles reified by the upper middle class and its supporting government that treat the individual as an exchange object. Mallarmé's poetry enables the subject to achieve a degree of autonomy in the private and public spheres of language.

Mallarmé achieves the goal of art in Kristeva's theory to the extent that his poetry shatters the unified or atomistic subject produced by capitalist France in the late nineteenth century. This poetry is, however, unable to complete the second step in art's social function according to this theory, to construct a thetic position that would bring about a change in social relations. Lacking the sociohistorical content that would enable psychic conflict to perform a subversive function, *Igitur* and *A Throw of the Dice* create esoteric, elitist moments out of pre-Oedipal narratives. In other words, Mallarmé's poems demonstrate the psychic conflict constituting the subject, conflict that a capitalist ideology, based on a unified self, does not acknowledge. They do not, however, produce the narrative that would convey knowledge about familial and social class relations and enable a broad audience to imagine changing those relations. Here Kristeva demonstrates a lesson she has learned from Marx despite her rejection of Marxist political theory and its monolithic subject (137–39). She describes the second part of art's goal, the part that Mallarmé does not achieve, in this way: "combining heterogeneous contradiction, whose mechanism the text possesses, with revolutionary critique of the established social order (relations of production—relations of reproduction): this is precisely what the dominant ideology and its various mechanisms of liberalism, oppression, and defense find intolerable" (190–91).

Mallarmé, along with Lautréamont, illustrate the Avant-garde's achievement, partial though it may be. Kristeva briefly theorizes how Joyce and Bataille are later able to write modern novels that, by constructing the ideological framework and sociohistorical content absent in Mallarmé's poems, mold pre-Oedipal conflicts into narratives representing social transformations as Cixous demonstrates in the case of Joyce. Thus, the Irish novelist will produce fiction representing the reality of familial and social class relations (in Kristeva's terms, "knowledge" and "socio-historical 'content,'" 187–88). Later, in *Time and Sense* (1994), Kristeva demonstrates in detail how Proust's *Remembrance of Things Past* also exemplifies the modern novel understood in this way.

Kristeva's complex theory of the psychic identifications played out in the text discovers a hidden dynamics in art and society as a whole. Her dialectical study of the subject's movements toward

mother and father in Mallarmé could be said to intervene in the evolution of literature and culture by revealing those movements. Kristeva's reading of the poet's emerging autonomy links his struggle to
that of the working class. Both poet and worker attempt to break with
the bourgeois capitalist psychic formation that denies the marginalized
status of the poor and of the child. Kristeva becomes engaged in another way by periodically locating versions of such psychic movements
in marginal writers, opening the canon to new additions Antoine De-
LaSale, Mikhail Bakhtin, and Jeanne Guyon are good examples.[12]

I have analyzed some of the moves that appear to undercut
both Kristeva's political interventions as described above and her
sense of literature's radical function. The dialectical methodology
that makes Kristeva's work a dynamic force in contemporary theory
also makes it seem vulnerable to charges that she is essentialist, neglects history, and reinforces gender stereotypes. Psychoanalytic writers in general possess a universalistic tendency seemingly open to
these charges. Situating individuals in the history of ideas, language,
and psychic formations, Kristeva as psychoanalytic theorist is not a
historian of political events or of social customs. She says very little
about the plight of the working class in nineteenth-century France,
for example, other than to draw a parallel between it and the situation of the Avant-garde poet, namely, that both are imprisoned by
upper-middle-class ideology. Also, like any statement differentiating
people on the basis of sex, race, religion, or social class her theory
seems to violate the individual's right to self-determination. Examples of this apparent violation include her discussion, on the one
hand, of the father presiding over the symbolic and demanding obe-
dience to the rules of language, and, on the other hand, of the
mother representing the semiotic and encouraging the subject to
break those rules. Beyond these theoretical moves that appear to undercut literature's radical function in Kristeva, some of her statements create a misleading context. In *Revolution*, she rejects Marxist
political theory for considering the subject monolithic (137–39).
The later volume, *Tales of Love*, similarly rejects the discipline that
has both attacked and supported gender stereotypes and essentialism, feminist theory. These statements mislead some readers who

fail to see Kristeva's overall sympathy with Marxism and feminism despite her critique of certain elements in these theories.

Thus, at times Kristeva seems to immobilize gender in definitions that give priority to the male, especially when she situates herself within a discussion that argues against political theory. She differentiates the roles of father and mother throughout her study of the work of art, stressing reunion with the mother to ensure its subversive thrust while at the same time demanding an identification primarily with the father to ensure its communicability. Kristeva connects this identification to the notion of a thetic position in *Revolution* and to that of the imaginary father in later works such as *Tales of Love* and *Black Sun*. Such definitions of male and female appear to provide the building blocks for an essentialist and biologist view of sexuality especially if combined with a third block, a subject periodically seeking reunion with the mother in a symbiotic "original" moment, as some readers perceive.[13]

These components of Kristeva's work make it seem vulnerable to the dangers of stereotyping and essentialism. The conflicting moves of her dialectical approach, however, imply not only an awareness of these dangers, but also a realization of the need to acknowledge their existence in fantasy and to confront them, as Jacquelyn Rose has said. In one of the best essays along with that of Toril Moi (in *Sexual/Textual Politics*) on Kristeva's theory, Rose discusses Kristeva's willingness to confront the problematic and masochistic side of the semiotic/feminine sometimes overlooked in feminist discussions. Rose points out that, far from being utopian, Kristeva's description of the attempted union with the mother often stresses psychic pain. In fact, subjectivity has both a feminine and masochistic component including pain, violence, and/or the death drive (*Sexuality*, 160). Violent action is frequently indicated in Kristeva's analyses of psychic formations by, for example, a "tearing away" or a "pulverizing" (*Revolution*, 51, 62). As Rose suggests in her discussion of Kristeva's use of the semiotic, her theory does not discredit feminism but instead helps make it a more complex and reflexive theoretical framework for approaching broad questions of subjectivity and politics (see chapters 3 and 4).

Kriteva confronts the power of stereotypes and essentialism at the moment when they surface in the conflicting movements toward both mother and father, for instance, in her analysis of Mallarmé. Considered as a whole, these movements are too complex to be described by the clear-cut male/female dichotomy characteristic of essentialist/biologist thought. The rejection of the mother is also a kind of union with her and an experience of pleasure (Kristeva uses the French psychoanalytic term *jouissance*). Disobeying the mother is really a disobeying of the father or movement toward a mother/father figure. The ambiguities of Kristeva's formulations cannot be contained within biologist concepts.

These formulations are not unlike Proust's in *Remembrance of Things Past* as chapters 2 and 3 make clear. Conflicting identifications with male and female figures emerge as his narrator struggles to become a writer. Proust confronts the question of sexual identity and of origins as does Kristeva. In the famous madeleine scene, for example, the narrator both assumes a female role and deprives the mother of her being. As he develops into a novelist, he will need to replay both male and female roles in an effort to return to an earlier experience of plenitude that is also a movement forward, a becoming.

A critical passage from the chapter on Mallarmé, "Freud's Notion of Expulsion: Rejection," helps make Kristeva's position on origins clearer. She is careful to point out that she is not positing a "first rejection" or original separation from the mother that sometimes serves as the cornerstone of essentialism:

> Rejection, or expenditure, constitutes the key moment shattering unity, yet it is unthinkable outside unity, for rejection presupposes thetic unity as its precondition and horizon, one to be always superseded and exceeded. Rejection serves to bind only to the extent that it is the precondition of the binding that takes place on another scene. To posit rejection as fundamental and inherent in every thesis does not mean that we posit it as origin. Rejection rejects origin since it is always already the repetition of an impulse that is

> itself a rejection. Its law is one of returning, as opposed
> to one of becoming; it returns only to separate again
> immediately and thus appear as an impossible forward
> movement. (147)

In this passage, she discusses the subject as always returning but never becoming, suggesting that the only change that is knowable is necessarily a repetition. She raises and confronts the problem of origin implicit in her theory of a reunion with the mother. While she does not fully explain the birth of subjectivity in the infant, she describes subjectivity as alive with contradictions, returning yet moving forward. Similarly, although she does not say exactly how change can emerge from repetition, she stresses change when she describes how rejection shatters and goes beyond unity and how returning is immediately followed by separation and forward movement.

The degree to which Kristeva's theory confronts essentialism becomes clearer not only in the refutation of origin but also in the discussion of Heraclitus as a source for the concept of rejection (156–57). Here she focuses on the ways in which rejection, growing out of Heraclitus's concept of reason, breaks free of logic to create a divided speech, a splitting of matter, and a shattering of reason itself ("the thetic logos"). All three events are marked by open-ended dialectical movements antithetical to the monolithic determinist movement of biologism that, whether in Aristotle or Hegel, always has a prescribed end in view.

In Kristeva, however, the subject's open-ended dialectical movements, a source for which she finds in Heraclitus, are not antithetical to a teleology. In fact, I have been arguing the very opposite. For her, psychoanalysis, employed in the treatment of patients and in the creation and analysis of works of art, includes a social function. In Ricoeur's terms, psychoanalysis, like Marxism, is "guided by the interest in emancipation"[14] or, in the terms I have been using, by the desire to shape the distribution of power in the family, government, and economy.

The thought-provoking questions that Kristeva's theory poses for subjectivity and its beginnings undercut and cause one to rethink not only oppositions like essentialism versus autonomy, as I have shown, but also the critical concepts of "author" and "text" that inform the response to literature. Philip Lewis immediately recognized *Revolution*'s contribution to literary theory in 1974.[15] A brief comparison of Kristeva's theory with that of other psychoanalytic readers of literature such as Jeffrey Mehlman reveals the impact of her understanding of the subject and narrative practice on the concepts of author and text. For Mehlman, on the one hand, the text is a formal literary structure with aesthetic unity. The author, in his view, sublimates desire in order to produce a coherent chef-d'oeuvre as part of a larger cultural and social order.[16] For Kristeva, on the other hand, the text is a narrative practice that periodically uses literary form to explode such categories as aesthetic unity. This practice only partly sublimates the desires of the subject who tells the story of psychic conflicts in familial, sexual, and historical scenarios. In narrating the process of his or her own coming into being, the subject breaks with communicative language and with the larger cultural order (or "social contract").

As the comparison with Mehlman indicates, Kristeva does not deny a role to aesthetic unity—a value in Western literature since Aristotle's *Poetics*—nor does she deny that the text's coherence is an integral part of the social order. On the contrary, she acknowledges both the way that familial/sexual relations bind literature and society together and the degree of coherence necessary for literature to be accessible and aesthetically pleasing to a reader. What Kristeva's theory does deny to more conservative psychoanalytic approaches to literature is the concept of an ultimately monolithic text representing a unified subject and supporting a society bent on maintaining the status quo.

In Kristeva, the subject's unruly drives liberate the text and the author. The text, for example, is freed of Aristotelian unity understood in an absolute sense, of the Cartesian dichotomy between "subject" and "object," and of ahistorical formalisms like American

New Criticism and French Structuralism. A *Throw of the Dice* or *Igitur* is no more an object than is Mallarmé himself: her theory of subjectivity deconstructs the subject-object dichotomy by showing how the subject's alternating identifications, or process of becoming, emerges in the text, making it function as a mobile series of discontinuous events. The conflicting movements toward both parents described above and in this passage can be seen as just such a series of discontinuous identifications:

> Oralization can be a mediator between the fundamental sadism of rejection and its signifying sublimation. Melody, harmony, rhythm, the "sweet," "pleasant" sounds and poetic musicality found in "symbolist" poetry and in Mallarmé, for example, may be interpreted as oralization. This oralization restrains the aggressivity of rejection through an attempted fusion with the mother's body, a devouring fusion: Mallarmé's biography documents this attempt. A return to oral and glottal pleasure combats the superego and its linear language, which is characterized by the subject/predicate sequences of its syntagms. Suction or expulsion, fusion with or rejection of the mother's breast seem to be at the root of this erotization of the vocal apparatus and, through it, the introduction into the linguistic order of an excess of pleasure marked by a redistribution of the phonematic order, morphological structure, and even syntax: portmanteau [*sic*] words in Joyce and syntax in Mallarmé, for example. (153-54)

Beyond the devouring fusion with the mother's body documented in Mallarmé's biography, the events described here, especially the oralization dramatizing the identification with the mother and the syntax reliving the movement toward the father, occur within a sociohistorical framework including the family and the state. Thus, Mallarmé's poems subvert patriarchal authority through maternal identification and the use of syntax. A *Throw of the Dice* and *Igitur* ultimately help undermine that framework. Kristeva makes clear that the poems uncover the late nineteenth century upper-middle-class ideology repressing the subject's psychic conflicts as well as the conflicts between middle class and workers. In other words, psychic and literary phenomena have a significant impact on the sociohistorical context, both public and private. For Kristeva, literature, including that of the *symbolistes*, cannot be understood as an example of ahistorical formalism. By writing narratives that include historical context, novelists such as Joyce and Proust (see chapters 2 and 3) will later reveal the connections among psychic, familial, and class conflict and the ways in which psychic confrontations underlie social hierarchies and inequitable power relations.

In conclusion, for Kristeva, literary form reveals the dynamics of a subject-in-process. Embedded in ideology and a sociohistorical context, he or she is very much a subject-in-the-world. More radically discontinuous than the Sartrean *pour-soi* because not fully synthesized within consciousness, the subject can move forward in unpredictable creative directions.

2

A Politics of Desire:
Reading Proust with Kristeva

Desire in Language: A Semiotic Approach to Literature and Art, a collection of Kristeva's work between 1969 and 1977, explores a wide variety of writers and painters including Roman Jakobson, Velimir Khlebnikov, Vladimir Mayakovsky, Antoine DeLaSae, Mikhail Bakhtin, Samuel Beckett, Roland Barthes, Louis-Ferdinand Céline, Giotto, and Giovanni Bellini.[1] Kristeva brings little-known writers to light, re-interprets many classic works, and reconsiders literary and art history with an awareness of the way dialogic aesthetic form shapes relations of power. Reading Marcel Proust's *Remembrance of Things Past* (*A la recherche du temps perdu*), in light of *Desire in Language* gives a fuller understanding of Proust's social critique and of Kristeva's sense of the social function of literature and painting as a break with the social contract.

Kristeva's early appreciation (in 1969) of Bakhtin as a writer at the crossroads of Russian Formalism, Marxism, and psychoanalysis is a good example, as I will show, of her ability to identify and explicate little-known, subversive, transitional figures. In 1974, Kristeva drew attention to several other significant Russian writers who were not widely known in Europe and the United States: Roman Jakobson, who worked with the Prague School after leaving Moscow in

1920, and the poets Khlebnikov and Mayakovsky ("The Ethics of Linguistics" in *Desire in Language*). The analysis of DeLaSale like that of Jeanne Guyon in the later volume *Tales of Love* introduces a European to a broader audience. Her choice of writers reflects both her interest in the dialogic quality of their work and, not unrelated to the work, their marginalized position. The essays collected in *Desire in Language* also often make reference to women as a marginalized group (49–50, 164–66, "Motherhood According to Bellini," 237–70). In 1974 as well, Kristeva wrote a controversial account of her trip to China that year, *About Chinese Women.*[2] In this volume, she examines a culture still little studied or understood by the rest of the world and gives special emphasis to the status of women in both China and the West (I discuss this in chapter 5).

Like Kristeva, Proust has sometimes been seen as writing in a conservative tradition. For many critics, as I document, Proust withdrew from the world, alienated by the crassness of the haute bourgeoisie, and created an elitist, Symbolist text. In light of Kristeva's early theory as I see it, *Remembrance*'s radical political discourse emerges in clear definition. She herself reads Proust later in *Time and Sense* (*Le Temps sensible*, 1994) where she shows how *Remembrance* develops out of Christian and Freudian concepts of love. In this later context to which I return in my final chapter on her most recent work, *Time and Sense* demonstrates that Proust's critique of the French beau monde grows out of and also helps to shape a sadomasochistic relationship to the mother. The narrator punishes her for being overly demanding while at the same time punishing himself to merit her love. Thus, as Kristeva points out, a sense of evil comes to be associated with love within the Christian tradition frequently alluded to in *Remembrance*.

In *Desire in Language*, as in her later theory, Kristeva's methodology is formalist and psychoanalytic, but unlike that of many academic critics trained in French Structuralism, or earlier in American New Criticism, her method neither separates formal and social functions nor relegates the latter to a secondary status. Rather, the study of the text's form is the necessary point of departure in explicating its politics.

Kristeva sees the text as an unleashing of unconscious drives, a liberation of innovative, instinctual discourse from traditional, communicative language. Building on the work of Freud, Bakhtin, and Lacan, Kristeva analyzes this liberation in terms of a break with the social contract. The text constitutes the life of the speaking subject who exists as a sequence of different selves: narrator, but also reader, addressee, and characters. In the creative act, the artist liberates the unconscious subject, and in so doing, breaks with the tradition of rational discourse in the West built on the assumption of a homogenous, logical self.

Following Kristeva, who discusses verbal texts in eight of the ten essays included in *Desire in Language*, this chapter focuses primarily on literature. Her theory sometimes transcends the boundaries of literature, as my discussion on Bellini later in this chapter makes clear. In literary texts, rational discourse denotes more than it connotes, and fuses one proposition to the next with causal links, leading to a conclusion already implied in the opening proposition. This essentially static structure, the thought pattern of a human being who is supposedly primarily rational, mirrors the Christian God and possesses a transcendent quality.

By partially liberating the speaking subject from rational discourse, literature frees him or her from the social structure that this discourse also reflects. In Kristeva, moving from linguistic conservatism (language as communication where denotation and logically linked propositions dominate) to sociopolitical conservatism (preservation of the status quo in capitalist or socialist structures) is not an unjustified leap because in every literary text, the inguistic is invariably sociopolitical to some extent, as Ricoeur suggests in his discussion of psychoanalysis, the social sciences, and Habermas (see chapter 1, p. 13).

The rational text repeatedly circulates words as objects of exchange and supports the privileged position of a unitary self within a logical, self-regulating economy. In such a text the self tries to deny the subject's need to negate and to accommodate the unorthodox unconscious drives that lead to change. Kristeva dramatizes the subject's need for negation and change. Giving less attention to theme, content, and denotation, she instead studies the dynamic interplay between two kinds of language: symbolic or communicative (in which theme dominates) and semiotic or instinctual. She uses the distinction between these two languages to explain how literature becomes a privileged form of human existence because it is in this form that we no longer repeat words and images into which the cogito is again fixed but rather create a new language into which the repressed life of the instincts is projected. This new language is defined in opposition to that in which logically connected clauses and denotation are primary. Instinctual language highlights connotations and creates patterns that are more rhythmical than logical, as she shows in her study of the Russian Futurist poets Khlebnikov and Mayakovsky in "The Ethics of Linguistics" (23–35).

Among the French and American critics who discuss Kristeva's work at any length, several dismiss or reject its politics. Her difficult dialectical methodology may help explain why they do not recognize its radical political thrust.[3] Kristeva's elliptical style, along with the analysis of subtle linguistic structures, deals with the issue of social change only indirectly and in the context of complex figures such as Hegel and Lacan. Furthermore, as I indicate in my analysis of *Revolution of Poetic Language* (see chapter 1, p. 19), a psychoanalytic methodology and the critique of Marxist political theory lead Kristeva's readers to misinterpret her politics. They see her work as universalist and conservative when it is actually sympathetic to Marxism although not uncritical, for example, of Marx's notion of a monolithic subject.

Philip Lewis's review article on *Revolution of Poetic Language* also treats some of the essays translated in *Desire in Language*.[4] An early introduction to Kristeva written in English recognizing the centrality of the political in her work, it calls attention to her understanding of the sociopolitical function of the avant-garde but fails to discuss this function at any length. For Lewis, the connection she makes between poetic process and political program is "problematic" and "susceptible to misunderstanding." He implies that because Kristeva's politics is restricted to the sphere of writing and to a writing that is marginal and inaccessible to a large audience, it does not merit extended treatment.

Claude Bouché's remarks on the sociopolitical aspects of Kristeva's work are pragmatic and reductive but such readings merit discussion because they have unfortunately often made it difficult for social and physical scientists to have a productive dialogue on psychoanalytic theory with those in the humanities. In his article "Materialist Literary Theory in France, 1965–1975," Bouché follows an orthodox Marxist line as he attempts to deflect the subversive thrust of her work in one short paragraph that condemns Kristeva along with all of the *Tel Quel* and *Change* writers as idealist.[5] Bouché rejects the work of *Tel Quel* and of any criticism that does not concentrate on the direct, concrete relationship between text and means of production. From a position that ignores the subtleties of language that Freud understands so well, including multiple meanings of words and the role of context in framing and creating meaning, he resembles American positivists whose pragmatism blinds them to the achievements of psychoanalysis.[6] When confronted by a rejection similar to Bouché's at a conference in Milan in 1973 on psychoanalysis and politics, Kristeva underlined the necessity to move beyond orthodox Marxism (and orthodoxy in general) and the study of the direct rapport between text and economic production. As in *Revolution of Poetic Language*, she reaffirms the political function of literature in her theory by explaining that a psychoanalytic approach demonstrates the impasse represented by forms of class society and opens up the possibility of moving beyond such forms.[7]

A reading of *Desire in Language* supports Kristeva's affirmation of a political function in literature if this function is understood as a shaping of the psychic formations that in turn have an impact on social institutions as Paul Ricoeur points out. Kristeva's formalism can be considered a radical political theory to the extent that it is a form of writing focused on emancipation, as Ricoeur describes. In this context, her theory also dramatizes the subject's need for upheaval of the social order. A study of this dramatization reveals her debt to Freud, Bakhtin, and Lacan. She derives many concepts central to her formalism from them. She imports Bakhtin's notion that linguistic forms possess the capacity to subvert. From Lacan (and from Bakhtin again as indicated below), she borrows the notion of literature as the text of the speaking subject who is inherently multi-ple. *Desire in Language* combines these concepts to build an eclectic theory in which linguistic, psychoanalytic, and political functions are integrally related, and puts the theory into practice in its discussions of literature and painting. Kristeva's "Word, Dialogue, and Novel" is a good example. Like the other essays on literature in the volume, it formulates a theory of the text as a series of alternations between instinctual and communicative language. Kristeva dramatizes these alternations by expressing them in terms of the subject's violent movements against or through a stable barrier that is the law or other defense of social structure.

The subject of the essay "Word, Dialogue, and Novel" is Bakhtin's notion of "the dialogic" deriving from Menippean satire and carnivalesque forms. Kristeva transforms this notion into the structuring principle of all texts understood within her eclectic theory:

> In other words the dialogism of Menippean and carnivalesque discourses, translating a logic of relations and analogy rather than of substance and interference, stands against Aristotelian logic. From within the very interior of formal logic, even while skirting it, Menippean dialogism contradicts it and points towards other forms of thought. Indeed, Menippean discourse develops in times of opposition against Aristotelianism, and writers of polyphonic novels seem to disapprove of the very structures of official thought founded on formal logic. (85)
>
> The poetic word, polyvalent and multideter-mined, adheres to a logic [the dialogic] exceeding that of codified discourse and fully comes into being only in the margins of recognized culture. Bakhtin was the first to study this logic, and he looked for its roots in carnival. Carnivalesque discourse breaks through the laws of language censored by grammar and semantics and, at the same time, is a social and political protest. There is no equivalence, but rather, identity, between

challenging official linguistic codes and challenging official law. (65)

In these telling passages, Kristeva underlines literature's sociopolitical dimension—it "challenges official law" and "disapproves of the very structures of official thought." For readers unfamiliar with Bakhtin, these statements appear simply to posit this dimension. For those who know his writings, it is difficult to see how challenging linguistic laws is identical to challenging governmental law—Ricoeur's analysis seems to go as far as equivalence but not identity unless one understands Ricoeur like Bakhtin to be examining the psychic formations underlying the response to both kinds of law. Kristeva builds on Bakhtin and assumes his understanding of literature as a political act that, in and through the linguistic forms constituting psychic structures, subverts the hierarchical tendencies of exterior social structure including both Western class societies and Stalin's rigid form of socialism.[8] For Bakhtin, Rabelais is a transitional figure who bridges the gap between the Middle Ages and the Renaissance. His work deconstructs the official values of feudalism's elite, particularly its belief in a transcendent God, by pitting them against the marginalized values of the people, that is, material existence and change. In Bakhtin's version of Rabelais, everything of value is likened to a hardy physical entity that grows.

While the source for Kristeva's conception of the political and linguistic levels of the text is Bakhtin, the source for her understanding of the psychoanalytic level, for the notion of a multiple subject who alternately constructs and dissolves structures that are at one and the same time linguistic and ideological, is again Bakhtin and more directly Lacan. Convinced of the validity of his notion of the subject, she reads Bakhtin as a precursor of Lacan, the imaginative interpreter of Freud: "In order to describe the dialogism inherent in the denotative or historical word, we would have to turn to the psychic aspect of writing as trace of a dialogue with oneself (with another), as a writer's distance from himself, as a splitting of the writer into subject of enunciation and subject of utterance" (74). In fact, Bakhtin is widely thought to be V. N. Volosinov who wrote *Freudianism: A Marxist Critique*, a work that, while indicating the limits of Freud's work, also recognized his importance.[9]

This passage shows how Kristeva understands the psychoanalytic level of the text to support the formal and sociopolitical levels. It suggests the way in which she puts her theory into practice. Part of the rhetoric she employs to dramatize linguistic and social upheaval as violent action against or through a stable barrier, the image of the "splitting of the writer" goes beyond its conventional use in psychoanalytic criticism. In this case, the barrier is the human being understood in traditional terms as a unitary self whose resistance to such action is felt in repeated reference to this self ("with oneself," "a writer's," "the writer," "subject of enunciation").

Other examples of the rhetoric that describes action against a barrier abound throughout her work. In the section in which she relates Saussure's concept of the poetic paragram to Bakhtin's dialogism, she states that the latter "implies a categorical *tearing from the norm* and a relationship of nonexclusive opposites" (71; emphasis added).[10] Here, as is often the case, the barrier under attack has both linguistic and social connotations—it is described as a kind of legislative authority, "the norm." Similarly, in the passage quoted above (65), "carnivalesque discourse *breaks through* the *laws* of a language *censored* by grammar and semantics and, at the same time, is a social and political protest." Variations of this rhetoric include "opening up" of an "enclosure" (26, 33), "bursting" or "clashing" movement (225), "shattering" of a surface (23, 261), and "transgression" (65, 70). The "shattering" of a surface, for instance, is often the form taken by the subject's negating energies in Kristeva's analysis of both Bakhtin's dialogism ("syntactic and semantic unity are shattered by the voices and accents of the 'others'") and Jakobson's innovations in linguistics and his commentary on the Russian Futurists, Mayakovsky and Khlebnikov: "*a code* (mores, social contract) *must be shattered* in order to give way to the free play of negativity, need, desire, pleasure, and jouissance, before being put together again, although temporarily and with full knowledge of what is involved" (23).

Kristeva's rhetoric serves to dramatize her theory of the text as revolutionary praxis and to lend coherence and conviction to this theory. Along with the images of violent action opposing a barrier are related images that belong to Freud and that depict the barrier as a watchman at a threshold (24, 27), or a screen that blocks the subject's speech (25). Kristeva uses Freud's images in conjunction with Lacan's notion of the decentered subject in ways that appear to read Freud and Lacan into texts in which a theory of the unconscious is at most only implicit, like Bakhtin's books on Rabelais and Dostoevsky and Jakobson's essays on the Russian Futurists. Kristeva's own rhetoric, and particularly the way in which she projects herself as Lacanian critic onto the text she analyzes, indicates a break with authoritarian critical stances that attempt to be primarily rational. As I have discussed more fully elsewhere, her rhetoric itself supports the thesis that language constitutes the linguistic and political liberation of the "speaking subject."[11]

By projecting herself onto the text she analyzes and by making her central theme unorthodox, semiotic discourse, Kristeva gives language a privileged position in her work. Revealing the charges of idealism and elitism to be misguided, she performs a political act by breaking with the social contract thematically and linguistically in her own "subjective" discourse and also, following from her theory, by giving individuals and groups considered marginal in the hierarchies of literary history a privileged role as well. Her complex analysis of a little-known prose piece of the fifteenth century, DeLaSale's *Jehan de Saintré*, for instance, sees it as central in the birth of the Realist European novel. She demonstrates how *Jehan* breaks with earlier prose, which restricted meaning to universals and avoided paradox in order to construct a feudal worldview. In the Realist novel, language becomes an open-ended material structure combining contradictions.

Kristeva's analysis of the role of the Lady makes clear that *Jehan de Saintré* is a very early example of this open-ended structure. Moving beyond feudalism to a capitalist ideology, DeLaSale combines the medieval idealized woman with an unfaithful paradoxical one: "Neither deified nor ridiculed, neither mother nor mistress, neither enamored of Saintré nor faithful to the Abbot, the Lady becomes the nondisjunctive figure par excellence in which the novel is centered."[12] Here Kristeva suggests that the rise of the realistic novel parallels that of the bourgeoisie and capitalism that shapes woman into an other whose value resides in her various uses as exchange object. While the Lady first appears to be the traditional inaccessible figure of courtly love, she soon becomes an undecipherable sensual being filled with ambiguities, especially in her encounter with the Abbot.

In the process of uncovering a social function in art, Kristeva reveals that the dynamics of form are both complex and specific. Her analysis of Saussure's *Anagrams* and DeLaSale's *Saintré*, for instance, could not be criticized for either oversimplifying or overgeneralizing problems of linguistic structure (poetic logic in the first volume, the birth of the realistic novel in the second). Part of the value of her formal method lies in the fact that she deals successfully with the particular elements of different works and disciplines, especially, in this volume, literature and painting. The dialectical interplay between the communicative and the instinctual that emerges in her analysis of texts manifests itself differently in her essays on Medieval and Renaissance painting, "Giotto's Joy" and "Motherhood According to Bellini." In the essay on Bellini, she projects herself with him onto the baby on the canvas whose desire for the mother, the search for jouissance, transforms the two-dimensional madonna into a play of color that creates a sense of volume or third dimension. Such desire is not for the traditional madonna whose identity is firmly connected to the baby whom she nourishes. Instead Kristeva describes this love in terms of the formal elements of the painting in which traditional representation in two dimensions (madonna and child as a phallic attempt to reach the mother) is deconstructed by the madonna's otherworldly, alienated, and characterless face and the almost abstract use of blocks of color for the human figures (247).

The dialectical movement from representation to its deconstruction functions as a political act as well as a formal procedure: representation, using "madonna and child" in the orthodox manner, reproduces the Renaissance humanist ideology that makes a fetish of the mother. She becomes the sexual object who is child oriented and "the seat of social conservation" (237). By subverting that ideology and the society that is sustained by it, Bellini liberates the subject and particularly the female subject. The chapter on Bellini makes clear that Kristeva's theory is materialist as well as feminist. It is feminist because for Kristeva to resist the use of the signs of communication for representing women constitutes a rejection of the so-called normal resolution of the Oedipal conflict. Here her example is Bellini's painting of the madonna and child. The artist in this context resists the roles of mother and heterosexual object that society imposes on the woman:

> The faces of his Madonnas are turned away, intent on something else that draws their gaze to the side, above, or nowhere in particular, but never centers it on the baby. Even though the hands clasp the child and bodies sometimes hug each other, the mother is only partially present (hands and torso), because, from the neck up, the maternal body not covered by draperies—head, face, and eyes—flees the painting, is gripped by something other than its object. (247)

Here, the unconscious projects itself into an antisocial antirepresentational feminine role and frees itself from authority. Ricoeur's theory is once again relevant: psychoanalytic theory, like the social sciences, recognizes the force of self-understanding and focuses on emancipation. One of its goals is to lift repression, to bring banished components of discourse back into the public sphere and in so doing, to redistribute power.[13]

Kristeva's early theory, including her analysis of Bellini, helps develop a fuller understanding of *Remembrance*, especially together with Serge Doubrovsky's reading of Proust, *The Place de la Madeleine*. Like Bellini's paintings, as Kristeva's and Doubrovsky's analyses combine to suggest, Proust's work presents a clear example of the rejection of the normal resolution of the Oedipal conflict.

On the one hand, critics as diverse as Germaine Brée, Georges Poulet, Jean-Pierre Richard, and René Girard, among others, for a long time continued to approach *Remembrance of Things Past* from a point of view originally taken by Edmond Wilson and Joseph Frank. They saw it as a conservative work enclosed within the tradition of the French Symbolist movement, *les symbolistes*.[14] According to that tradition, the writer withdraws from upper bourgeois society with its capitalist values and creates a text intended for an elite. Walter Benjamin, on the other hand, is keenly aware of Proust's distance from his aristocratic characters—"there is not one [of the problems of Proust's characters] which would be identical with those of the author"—and from the salon milieu he describes so well. Benjamin speaks of "the explosive power of Proust's critique of society" and states that Proust's concerns are "subversive."[15]

Without treating the subversive politics suggested in Benjamin and fundamental to Kristevan theory as I read it, Doubrovsky probes successfully beneath the conscious level of Proust's discourse in his extended psychoanalytic study of *Remembrance*.[16] One of the significant conclusions that he draws is that Proust's aesthetic is to be carefully distinguished from that of his narrator, as Benjamin implies. In this light, *Remembrance* should be seen as a novel that breaks with Symbolism.

Concentrating on the function of the bedtime and madeleine scenes, Doubrovsky demonstrates that the novel constitutes a frustrated quest for identity and a rejection of the usual resolution of the Oedipal conflict. In Proust, the narrator first unites with the mother in an attempt to satisfy a lack of identity (the bedtime scene). At a later stage of the conflict, he reverses the initial union, deprives the mother of her being (eats the madeleine), and attempts to establish a sense of self in his novel. According to Doubrovsky's analysis, the writing experience constitutes not the successful and jubilant quest for selfhood that his narrator would have us believe, but a painful and failure-ridden recognition that such selfhood is an illusion.

From the perspective of both Kristeva's early theory and Doubrovsky's criticism, the *Remembrance* constitutes a critique of the Symbolist aesthetic as an attempt to transform the fluctuating movements of the psyche into a homogenous linguistic object containing no reference to anything outside of its own coherent structure. While a different version of this aesthetic, as in the case of Mallarmé and Lautréamont in *Revolution of Poetic Language* (see chapter 1), might be seen to drive the psyche's fluctuations, in Kristeva's terms, "the semiotic," this is not so in *Remembrance*. Unlike these Symbolist poets who resist the French rational st tradition, Proust's narrator presses Symbolism into service as he struggles to establish a sense of self in the novel he is writing. In Proust, the narrator's Symbolist aesthetic serves the purposes of "symbolic discourse" to use Kristeva's words. Kristeva's early work provides a context to read Proust as a novelist of introspection and of emancipation from a Symbolist aesthetic. In fact, Proust himself had written a more direct critique of such an aesthetic back in 1896.[17]

From the perspective provided by Kristeva's early writing, *Remembrance* emerges as a liberating work that in part frees the subject from the narrator's Symbolist aesthetic and also from repressive class society. For Kristeva (influenced by but not in full agreement with Marx who sees political and economic structures as fundamental), as for Maurice Merleau-Ponty whose work she analyzes later in *Time and Sense*, and for Bakhtin and Ricoeur as I indicated earlier, the psychic mechanisms incorporated in writing clearly have an impact on political structures.

In *Remembrance*, the narrator's Symbolism, his efforts to reify the ephemeral, discontinuous, sensual experiences of his apprenticeship as a writer is one side of a double discourse. The other side negates these efforts by revealing them to be repressive—they deny instinctual drive and limit the subject's existence to a coherent linguistic structure without discontinuity. Moments of involuntary memory lose their fundamentally disruptive character and are made to appear to testify to a transcendent self. In the last section of the novel, the narrator often claims, for instance, that the madeleine and paving stone episodes reveal an unchanging core of being that the preceding 2,800 pages of discontinuous experiences deny.[18]

Like his attitude toward the theory of fiction, the narrator's view of salon society is double. On the one hand, it is the setting par excellence for art: he hears and discusses the fine Vinteuil sonata and meets Bergotte, the author he admires most, at the Verdurins.

The salon is, on the other hand and more often, the worst possible environment for art: objects and guests are chosen for their exchange value, that is, their prestige within the hierarchical upper class and not for their own merits. Swann, for instance, becomes one of the Verdurin clan not for any special virtue of his own, but because he is the friend of Odette who has been selected by the authoritarian Mme Verdurin as the fashionable *cocotte* of the season. Although he claims to be working on Vermeer, Swann has nothing of interest to say about the painter and actually works only occasionally on this project. For many years the narrator himself allows the beau monde to hinder his writing by devoting himself almost exclusively to the predominantly mindless repartee of the Guermantes salon. Proust delivers a critique of salon society as one that does not encourage the artistic individual but exploits and exchanges him as an object in order to maintain and solidify its privileged position within a hierarchy resistant to change.[19]

Proust demonstrates the inadequacies of his narrator's convictions concerning literature and society. His text splits into a dialectical sequence that alternately reifies and represses, or frees, the subject. That is to say, the orthodox language of Symbolism repeatedly takes shape and dissolves as the novel progresses. The most obvious dissolution of this language occurs during the moments of involuntary memory that force the narrator to recognize unconscious desire awakening pleasurable sensations linked to the past and disrupting his sense of self.

Such a moment occurs at the Guermantes matinée when Marcel wipes his mouth with a stiff napkin. A vision of blue transports him to the seashore at Balbec and fills him with joy. He feels that the butler who gave him the napkin had opened a window onto the sea inviting him to walk along the shore:

> and this napkin now, unfolded for me—concealed within its smooth surfaces and its folds—the plumage of an ocean green and blue like the tail of a peacock. And what I found myself enjoying was not merely these colors but a whole instant of my life on whose

> summit they rested, an instant which . . . caused me to
> swell with happiness. (901)

The napkin episode recreates a past moment at Balbec. Stiffness over the mouth, pleasure for the eyes, for the legs (an invitation to stroll), a feathery tail, a movement upward ("an aspiration toward . . . a summit," "to swell with happiness"): the experience is clearly sexual. Like the other moments of involuntary memory, this episode is an example of what Kristeva would call "semiotic discourse." A splitting of the conscious subject occurs, interrupting the Symbolist narrator's orthodox linear language and freeing him to pursue a forever-receding "original" moment.

These moments indicate that Symbolism's attempt to create a unitary self in language is a sham. The narrator describes the paving stone, spoon, and napkin episodes at the Guermantes matinée in terms that reveal his awareness of the inadequacies of Symbolism:

> But this species of optical illusion, which placed beside
> me a moment of the past that was incompatible with
> the present, could not last long . . . my recent experience
> of the three memories . . . instead of giving me a more
> flattering idea of myself, had almost caused me to doubt
> the reality, the existence of that self. . . . Fragments of
> existence withdrawn from Time: these then were perhaps
> what the being three times, four times brought
> back to life within me had just now tasted, but the contemplation,
> though it was of eternity, had been fugitive.
> (3:906, 908)

The emphasis on the episodes' artificial ephemeral character would suggest that although these episodes are in themselves very real and precious to him because they release unconscious drives, they cannot be considered proof of an unchanging core of being but rather of a fluctuating series of selves.[20]

The narrator's ambivalent aesthetic theory and his equally ambivalent attitude toward the salon appear to be separate phenomena.

They are actually closely linked in that both Symbolist text and beau monde function in ways that dehumanize by reifying the individual and by rendering him or her homogenous and closed to change. This link appears in the following passage, for instance, where, despite his regret, the writer's exploitation of the people he has known follows a pattern not unlike that which emerges in the salon:

> All those men and women who had revealed some truth to me and who were now no more, appeared again before me, and it seemed as though they had lived a life which had profited only myself, as though they had died for me. Saddening too was the thought that my love, to which I had clung so tenaciously, would in my book be so detached from any individual that different readers would apply it, even in detail, to what they had felt for other women. But had I a right to be shocked at this posthumous infidelity, shocked that strangers should find new and alien objects for my feelings in unknown women, when this infidelity, this division of love between a number of women, had begun in my life-time and even before I had started to write? It was true that I had suffered successively for Gilberte, for Mme de Guermantes, for Albertine. But successively I had also forgotten them, and only the love which I dedicated to different women had been lasting. (3:939–40)

Considering *Remembrance* in the context of Kristeva's work, this passage suggests that the narrator's program uses people, and especially women, no less than does salon society, as objects of exchange to support a unitary seat of authority, the Symbolist's self in the case of the narrator, the aristocracy or the haute bourgeoisie (the Guermantes or the Verdurins) in the case of the salon. Not unlike Kristeva's own use of repetition to convey the unitary self's resistance in her analysis of Bakhtin's dialogism (see p. 34), Proust's obtrusive and obsessive repetition of personal and possessive adjectives and pronouns, "me," "myself," "I," "my" portrays the ways in which this authoritarian presence commands attention.

Several other elements of *Remembrance* associate Symbolist text and salon and indicate that the first may be understood as a kind of metaphor for the second. In revealing the inadequacies of the narrator's Symbolist theory, *Remembrance* reveals at the same time the repressive nature of his milieu. The narrator uses this milieu (particularly the Guermantes salon) as the material out of which he will shape his delusive myth of identity, a Symbolist text, much as Swann uses the Verdurins to shape an equally delusive myth of identity, his love for Odette. The Guermantes matinée is the "setting" of the narrator's novel in more ways than one. As in a piece of jewelry, the old friends encountered there become precious stones that act as a foil to the transcendent self, the most precious stone in his work (3:974). Most importantly, the very presence of the salon (the paving stones in the Guermantes court, the spoon, and the napkin) jogs the narrator's memory and in this way eventually helps him to write.

Reading Proust with Kristeva sets *Remembrance* in perpetual motion as a kind of spinning top whirling through new versions of unified selves and discontinuous subjects. Paul DeMan identifies a similar mobile form in Proust when he describes the interplay of metaphor and metonymy in the novel as a "flight of meaning" whose own meaning is "incessantly in flight."[21]

Despite his Symbolist delusions, the narrator's self-portrait in the conclusion describes the novel's movement with a different precision. Instead of whirling like a top, for him the novel totters precariously back and forth. Not unlike the forward and backward temporal shifts of autobiographical fiction in general, Proust's double discourse as I described earlier alternately moves forward as the Symbolist narrator shapes past events into a future novel and moves backward as involuntary memory recreates "original" instants of pleasure. Marcel movingly talks about the life he wants to record in his book as lost in time. He sees himself as a kind of monster, like those around him (*des êtres monstrueux*) tottering back and forth pre-

cariously on stilts that continue to grow longer and longer pene-
trating deep into places visited years ago (3:1107) as he fights fa-
tigue, risks falling, and attempts to stay attached.

Kristeva's early theory is useful in repositioning Proust's un-
locatable "monster" in literary history. In light of her work, he does
not bring the Symbolist era to an elegant and elaborate culmina-
tion, but instead helps establish the new frontiers of psychoanalytic
writing and its radical social function.

3

Psychoanalysis, Feminism, and *Remembrance*

Kristeva's theory provides a foundation for a reading of Proust (begun in the preceding chapter) and more generally for feminism. Like De-Beauvoir's *The Second Sex* and Luce Irigaray's *Speculum of the Other Woman*, Kristeva's *Desire in Language* and *About Chinese Women* contribute to a theoretical foundation for feminism.[1] Bringing her neo-Freudian theory of semiotic language to bear on Western philosophy, literature, and art, *Desire in Language* and *About Chinese Women* constitute a critique of the symbol of the father, the authority at the center of consciousness in the French Rationalist tradition. Having lived in Bulgaria during her formative years (1941–66) and writing a theory whose oppositional nature is highlighted in chapters 1 and 2 of this book, Kristeva turns to Eastern models, Russian and Chinese, to launch her critique of the symbol of the father and of symbolic language in general in both volumes. At the same time, Kristeva de-emphasizes the impact of the figure of the father and focuses instead on sexual difference and the mother's role in these works.

In *Desire in Language*, she describes how art and society are inextricably linked. As I have shown in placing *Remembrance* in the context of the essays in *Desire in Language* (see chapter 2), significant psychic formations reveal themselves in the language underlying

Proust's novel and especially French salon society where individuals are exploited to support a hegemonic upper middle class. Kristeva uses the category of language in this collection of her essays (with "text," "writing," and "discourse" as varieties of language), as do many other French psychoanalytic theorists, such as Hélène Cixous, to discuss the dialectic of conscious and unconscious movements constituting art and society. In her essay on the Russian Futurist poets Khlebnikov and Mayakovsky in *Desire in Language*, the male takes the shape of the sun that is a threatening entity because it constricts the individual's life as a writer and social being. The sun is the agency of language that molds and limits the rhythmic physical and psychic life the poet tries to express in his writing. At the same time, this sun constitutes a "paternal law" and a "legislative seat," that is, a male entity that controls relations with others (including the family) and ensures the communicability of his poems.

Kristeva's meditative account of her 1974 trip to China, *About Chinese Women*, describes how the symbol of the father or unified male self—in Lacanian terms, the phallus or symbolic practice—dominates language in the West. Kristeva traces the figure of the male back to the monotheism and economic necessities of early Judaism (discussed at greater length in chapter 5 where I include a fuller examination of *About Chinese Women*). In contrast to Western practice, in China as Kristeva explains, Taoist traditions produce a more flexible language relatively free of the male figure's dominance. She discusses two additional sources for the development of such a language as an androgynous medium inflected more subtly by sexual difference. These two sources, the possible legacy of matriarchy, on the one hand, and Mao's programs, on the other, are controversial and have led to a heated debate on the accuracy and adequacy of Kristeva's historical perspective in light of China's persecution of its citizens and abuse of personal freedoms.

The category of the unconscious is central to Kristeva's understanding of art in her early essays (on the Futurists and on the Italian Renaissance painter Giovanni Bellini) and to Proust's novel. The unconscious disrupts the formal elements of art in such a way that it transforms the notion of the self as a fixed rational male entity produced by Western civilization and by French Rationalism in particular. What emerges from this transformation is a more corporeal, volatile subject that is not male. In the Futurists, for instance, not only does this subject oppose a male self, but also it takes on the form of a mother or virgin (30). In fact, Kristeva shows that the structure underlying Khlebnikov's and Mayakovsky's poems can be understood as an alternation between two personae:

> Khlebnikov evokes another aspect of this solar contest: a mother, coming to the aid of her children in their fight against the sun. The otter's children are squared off against three suns, one white, one purple, and the other dark green. In "God of the Virgins," the protagonist is "the daughter of the sun prince." The poem "Ka" calls for the "hairy-armed sun of Egypt." All of Khlebnikov's pagan mythology is underlain with a contest against the sun supported by a feminine figure, all-powerful mother or forbidden virgin, gathering into one representative and thus substantifying all that which, with Mayakovsky, hammered in sonorous thrusts within and against the system of language—that is, rhythm. (29–30)

The subject (mother, virgin, or poet) attempts to express the movements of unconscious, instinctual life, and the male self (paternal sun, apparent poet) tries to impose the fixity of language onto this life, much as Proust's narrator does. The discussion of Khlebnikov's and Mayakovsky's poetry is an example of the mother's role as an integral element in Kristeva's theory of literature. Representations of the mother and other female figures based on her dramatize the subject's physical life and pleasure. Such representations disrupt the power relations connecting the subject to others and to the social contract.

Kristeva's theory is at once both psychoanalytic and feminist. I am thinking of feminism as a philosophical movement broadly defined as the study of the category "woman" in an effort to understand, analyze, and oppose sexist practices. Kristeva's theory, often stressing the therapeutic effect of literature, indicates how the writing or reading process serves to lift repression and domination by the father. Her approach is feminist—despite her critique of some feminist theory—as well as psychoanalytic to the extent that the writer or reader breaks with a male authority figure and identifies with a female subject in the process, an identification prominent in Proust's work.[2] This break, as it appears in her discussion of the Russian Futurists and Bellini, for example, goes beyond the way in which literature and painting violate the rules of communication by multiplying signification or reference. The unconscious organization of the formal elements in art violates the notion of a male self that functions as the core of Western language and social structures dating back to at least Descartes in the French Rationalist tradition.

Kristeva explains this notion of the male self and the liberating identification with a female subject in the psychoanalytic contexts created earlier by Freud and Lacan. As in Freud's *Leonardo*, the reunion with the mother plays a fundamental role in Kristeva's theory.[3] She is referring primarily to the figure of the mother represented in Western cultures (see chapter 6 of this book) as explained in part by Jacques Lacan, as well as to the artist's real biological mother.

For Lacan, children learn to speak when they are wrenched from the mother and from the physical and psychological well being derived from an original connection to her.[4] At the onset of speech, the girl or boy identifies with the father as the authority figure in personal and public life. Learning to speak means entering a contract that recognizes the male self as the power underlying language and social structures. According to Kristeva, in breaking with language as society understands it, the writer rejects the contractual identifications with the father and experiences a reunion with the mother; in this way, contradictory though it seems, the poet recreates within writing a life that predates the mastery of language.

Kristeva establishes vital links between the work of art and the flow of unconscious experience that ultimately derives both physically and psychologically from the initial union enjoyed with the mother, as she shows in her analysis of Khlebnikov and Mayakovsky. Kristeva views the text as a process advancing dialectically in time through concrete linguistic structures. This view, along with her methodology, derives in part from Hegel (see the opening pages of chapter 1). I have shown that in Kristeva a dialectical process advances as an alternation or opposition between the communicative language of a unified self (the symbolic) and the irrational language of a volatile subject (the semiotic). The process may also be described as an opposition between male and female.

Because this dialectic implicitly connects the literary text and society by emphasizing the notion of a unified self underlying each, Kristeva's theory is sociopolitical. More specifically, her theory contains a feminist element that cannot be ignored despite its indirection and her own rejection of the "feminist" label (see chapter 5, p. 84). From Kristeva's point of view, literature liberates an unconscious, prerational life that human beings experience in their early stages in the attachment to the mother. Her theory helps provide a foundation for feminist criticism and for a feminist reading of Proust to the extent that it incorporates woman's experience into literature: the union between mother and child that, both literally and figuratively, is a fundamental aspect of the human situation recreated in literary language.

Although he never discusses the sociopolitical and feminist implications of Kristeva's theory as a context for Proust, Serge Doubrovsky focuses on the quest for the mother and analyzes the narrator's attempt to liberate himself from a repressive unified self.[5] The preference for the maternal name Marcel over the paternal Proust[6] mirrors the liberation he seeks in identifying with a variety of female subjects—Tante Léonie, grandmother, Albertine (and, as I will show, Françoise, and the apparently male Saniette)—and in rejecting the male self formerly assumed in the bedtime scene.

Kristeva's theory and methodology illuminate and support my interpretation of the novel as a critique of one model of the French Symbolist Movement and of the phallocentric foundation upon which it is based and which it in turn helps support. In light of Kristeva, the narrator's identifications with the servant, Françoise, and the paleographer, Saniette, go beyond the conventional doubling of self that psychoanalysis sees in the figures of dreams and literature.

There are moments, as I will show, when these characters, part of the narrator's symbolic discourse, function instead as a subversive, semiotic discourse in which the subject seeks an "original" experience of pleasure.

Despite the fact that critics have written volumes on Proust's novel, they have not treated Françoise and Saniette at any length. Nor have they discussed in any substantial way the connections between these characters and the central focus of Proust's novel as a form of radical social criticism. Without treating *Remembrance* at length, the Russian critic Mikhail Bakhtin (see chapter 2) provides insights into character (including Françoise) and point of view in Proust.[7] Other readers have also sensed Françoise's importance. Walter Benjamin, for instance, has noticed a kind of identification with the flattery and curiosity of servants in Proust's writing.[8] Others have noticed that she is the only character who, along with Charlus, "provides the continuous perception of a living duration in Proust." They have written, for example, that "Françoise and Charlus alone would assure Proust's fame as novel-ist," that "she is the most clearly female character in the novel," and that as "a representative of the people" she bears "the wisdom of the common folk and . . . holds the correct attitude toward life and death."[9] The fact that many critics, on the one hand, writing in the traditions of French Structuralism and American New Criticism, focus on the novel's form isolated from its social commentary and psychic explorations may help explain the lack of attention paid to Françoise and Saniette. In light of Kristeva's theory and criticism, the *Recherche*, on the other hand, links form to psychic exploration and social criticism.

It is not surprising, given Bakhtin's own ability to connect literary, social, and psychic structures, that Kristeva was among the first in the West to discover him. For Bakhtin, one way novelists undermine the social system is by creating characters who, like Françoise, "represent the people." He traces these representatives back to characters from folklore who perform productive labor and hold attitudes toward fundamental aspects of human experience (death, food, drink, love, childbirth) that are absent for the most part in contemporary ruling classes. According to Bakhtin, novelists such as Proust are often able to expose the deceit and inhumanity underlying the myths created by the ruling classes by means of these representatives who possess a healthy failure to understand such myths.

Informed by Kristeva, my reading of Proust highlights the sociopolitical significance of the psychological and aesthetic and, in particular, the significance of the narrator's identifications with females. Proust's work offers an implicit criticism of not only Symbolism, but also of the exploitation of women in the beau monde. Rather than strengthening woman's marginal position as salon entertainment—a position that Odette occupies for the Verdurins, for example—Proust reveals the inhumanity of the politics that places her there. He elevates woman by associating her with the artistic process, as both Kristeva's theory of the semiotic and Serge Doubrovsky's analysis of the series of female identifications in *The Place de la Madeleine* show. This process is opposed to the narrator's Symbolist theory and to the functioning of salon society in general (see chapter 2). Several passages, such as the following, indicate the role of women as exchange objects in the narrator's conception of art:

A work, even one that is directly autobiographical, is at the very least put together out of several intercalated episodes in the life of the author—earlier episodes which have inspired the work and later ones which resemble it just as much, the later loves being traced after the pattern of the earlier. For the woman whom we have loved most in our life we are not so faithful as we are to ourself, and sooner or later we forget her in order—since this is one of the characteristics of that self—to be able to begin to love again. At most our faculty of loving has received from this woman whom we so loved a particular stamp, which will cause us to be faithful to her even in our infidelity. We shall need, with the woman who succeeds her, those same morning walks or the same practice of taking her home every evening or giving her a hundred times too much money. (3:945–46)

The authority figure makes its presence felt in the male writer's exploitation of the women he has loved in order to write and enjoy subsequent women. As the stuff of writing and the source of future pleasure, the woman is dehumanized, reduced to an image to be traced, a set of habits to be repeated, an economic dependent to be patronized. In light of Kristeva's analysis of the feminine, the idea of being "faithful to her even in our infidelity" suggests that the narrator's womanizing is a defense against her influence and that the primary identification with the mother is not recognized and accepted emotionally.

This passage can be seen as a kind of microcosm of *Remembrance*: it alludes to the bedtime and Madeleine scenes ("several intercalated episodes in the life of the author—earlier episodes which have inspired the work and later ones which resemble it just as much"). As in the passage, in the bedtime episode, on the one hand, the woman becomes the victim, the child becomes the adult male whose pleasure necessitates the suppression of her will: "this return to humane conditions which . . . raised me to the dignity of a grown-up person, brought me of a sudden to a sort of puberty of sorrow . . . if I had just won a victory, it was over her that I had succeeded . . . in relaxing her will . . . she would prefer to let me enjoy the soothing pleasure of her company (1:41). In the Madeleine scene, on the other hand, as in subsequent scenes where the narrator identifies with female figures, no such victimization of the woman occurs. Although he remains unaware of it, in the process of drinking the tea and eating the cake, he assumes a female role. His pleasure does not suppress that of the other person but rather leads to the birth of his childhood memories and eventually of his book: "a shudder ran through me and I stopped, intent upon the extraordinary thing that was happening to me. An exquisite pleasure had invaded my senses . . . this new sensation having had in me the effect which love has of filling me with a precious essence" (1:48). Unlike the passages describing the bedroom drama and the exploitation of women in writing, here the narrator relives the mother's jouissance and participates in her life-giving role. In this sense, he no longer sets up a defence mechanism but instead accepts a primary identification with her. In the context of *Remembrance*, viewed as a series of identifications with female figures like the mother in this quotation, the earlier passage on women and literature can be read ironically as an implicit critique of Symbolism, the beau monde, and the Rationalist traditions from which they spring.

The narrator's identification with Françoise, probably his best known "representative of the people," reveals the variety of ways in which the novelist points a finger at exploitative relationships, particularly those of the narrator himself, engaged in Symbolist writing and salon society. Françoise serves as both a positive and a negative example in Proust's critique of salon life and espouses mixed attitudes toward the well-to-do. These attitudes appear in the opening of *The Guermantes Way* where she has just moved into the new Parisian apartment along with the narrator's family. She repeatedly expresses a longing for her previous life in Combray, a preference for the small village of her birth over the grand French capital in terms that clearly pit peasant and middle-class life against that of the beau monde and the narrator:

> Ah, Combray, when will I see you again, poor old place? When will I spend the whole blessed day among your hawthorns, under our own poor lilac trees, hearing the finches sing and the Vivonne making a little noise like someone whispering, instead of that wretched bell from our young master, who can never stay still for half an hour on end without having me run the length of that blessed corridor. . . . Ah, if only I had a crust of dry bread to eat and a faggot to keep me warm in winter, I'd have been back home long since in my brother's poor old house at Combray. Down there at least you feel you're alive; you don't have all these houses stuck up in front of you, and there's so little noise at night-time you can hear the frogs singing five miles off and more. . . . Yes, with Mme Octave—ah, a real saintly woman, I can tell you, and a house where there was always more than enough, and all of the very best—a good woman, and no mistake, who

didn't spare the partridges, or the pheasants, or anything. You might turn up five to dinner or six, it was never the meat that was lacking, and of the first quality too, and white wine, and red wine, and everything you could wish. . . . It was she that always paid the damages, even if the family stayed for months and years. (2:12, 19, 21)

At first glance, the servant repeats the clichéd idyllic nostalgia for country life. In the context of *Remembrance* considered as a critique of salon society and as a study of the birth of a writer, these passages reveal Proust's own values that directly oppose those of the salon society that constantly threaten the outsider, and particularly the artistic outsider. The words offer a sharp contrast between, on the one hand, Françoise's memories of Combray—natural beauty, quiet solitude, robust family meals—and, on the other hand, the life of the affluent in Paris—carefully decorated interiors, a cacophony of gossiping pontificating voices, salon gatherings of many people for the most part unrelated by family ties, and light refreshments like orangeade.

The finches, pigeons, frogs, Vivonne River, lilacs, and particularly the hawthorns echoing the *Combray* scene that made these flowers famous, reveal the power nature possesses to arouse the artist. The solitude and quiet underscored in these descriptions of the Combray countryside are crucial in the pursuit of art, as the narrator often reminds us as he struggles to limit his participation in the Guermantes soirées.

The family meals overflowing with the hearty fare of meats and wines paid for by Tante Léonie represent what is most fundamental in the narrator's childhood memories. The critical madeleine scene in the first volume reveals that it is out of these memories, awakened by the recollection of Tante Léonie's herb tea and cakes that his writing emerges—there is, after all, a time for lighter refreshment. A spokeswoman for the narrator in the above passage, Françoise opposes Combray to the Paris that prevents him from becoming a writer for so long, and that more generally, is hostile to the well-being and development of the individual (Swann is another good example). The arbitrary power wielded by wealthy Parisians appears in the image Françoise paints of the young master constantly ringing for his servant. Suffering at the hands of others in Paris, she is free to take walks and enjoy the countryside in Combray.

A study of the passage reveals the narrator identifying with Françoise and recreating two moments of involuntary memory: the hawthorn episode and the madeleine scene. "Ah, Combray, when will I see you again, poor old place? When will I spend the whole blessed day among your hawthorns . . . ?" voices Marcel's desire for the earlier moment of pleasure outdoors. Simple terms such as "*pauvre terre*" (poor old place) link the peasant closely to the young boy the narrator is trying to awaken in himself. "Yes, with Mme Octave—ah, a real saintly woman, I can tell you, and a house where there was always more than enough, and all of the very best . . . and everything you could wish," affirms the complete satisfaction enjoyed in the madeleine scene in straightforward language typical of servants and children and not without sexual allusions. In the context of the earlier hawthorn and madeleine scenes, episodes like this one with Françoise resonate with associations to the narrator's intimate experiences. In Kristeva's terms, such episodes can be read as part of Proust's semiotic discourse recreating union with the mother. The passage is, in fact, replete with female sexual allusions: "Combray" is pronounced like "Conbray" in French with "con" the equivalent of "cunt"; Françoise imagines herself under sweet-smelling trees, running the length of a corridor, with a faggot to keep her warm, and so on.

A Françoise very different from the one who bemoans Parisian life can be seen mistreating the chickens and the kitchen maid in Combray. The use of power to threaten the individual in the aristocratic and upper bourgeois world of the Guermantes, the Verdurins, and the narrator is no less obvious in the working class. The cruel treatment of the sick kitchen maid who is forced to suffer for more than an hour while Françoise sobs over the theoretical discussion of the maid's symptoms in a medical handbook (1:134) is a good example of how Proust uses the head servant as a negative model. Not satisfied with such cruelty, Françoise decides to serve asparagus nearly everyday that summer once she discovers that cleaning them triggers the maid's asthma attacks.

Like his head servant who chooses the verbal world of medical books and newspapers to escape from the suffering of individuals, the narrator chooses a mode of writing that, in one of its variations, allows him to deny both his public and private experience of change and death, the mode of the Symbolist. Like Françoise, too, the narrator, though not an aristocrat or sufficiently wealthy to be a member of the haut bourgeois elite, internalizes the exploitative attitudes of these classes and attempts to feed parasitically on others to sustain himself as an intellectual who is welcome in the beau monde. His treatment of both Françoise and Albertine are instances of this attempt. The narrator's description of Françoise turns back on itself and reveals the inadequacy of not only his servant's values but also his own, particularly vis-à-vis Symbolist literature and the salon.

Discussing the joyful episodes of involuntary memory that he will transform into writing, the narrator declares:

> I experienced them at the present moment and at the same time in the context of a distant moment, so that the past was made to encroach upon the present and I was made to doubt whether I was in the one or the other. . . . This explained why it was that my anxiety on the subject of my death had ceased at the moment when I had unconsciously recognized the taste of the little Madeleine, since the being which at that moment I had been was an extra-temporal being and therefore unalarmed by the vicissitudes of the future. (3:871)

The moments of involuntary memory are primarily disruptive and give evidence of the flux of subjective states in this passage—he cannot decide initially whether it is present or past time that he is experiencing. In the final episodes at the Princesse de Guermantes' reception, the narrator denies their disorienting effect and claims that they testify to a transcendent self (see chapter 2, p. 39). Yet, in light of Kristeva's theory, the narrator's disoriented state during the moments of involuntary memory do not demonstrate the existence of a transcendent self successfully recreated in a Symbolist text. The ephemeral quality of the narrator's experience and the anguish he suffers in the face of death and other sources of change reveal the repression dictated by this aesthetic. Like the French Rationalist traditions of which it is a part, the narrator's version of Symbolism, unlike that of Mallarmé and Lautréamont (see chapter 1, p. 16), ends in failure.

His Symbolist theory denies autonomy not only to his own multiple and temporal existence but also to other people. The theory treats others as objects in order to create the authority figure that is the Symbolist self. Both Symbolism and salon use individuals to support such a figure: the Symbolist self in the case of the narrator, the aristocracy or haute bourgeoisie (the Guermantes or Verdurins) in the case of the salon (see chapter 2, p. 40).

A closer look at the narrator's relationship to Françoise reveals that the repressive nature of his theory extends to the production of his writing. She is exploited by the narrator in what is for the most part the master–slave relationship she herself describes (2:12). Yet, despite her low status as servant, her role in the narrator's apprenticeship as a writer is anything but marginal As Ramon Fernandez noticed long ago, she is present in most of the major episodes in the narrator's life—the bedtime scene and the final commentary on the narrator's book, to name just two. Many unflattering close-ups of Françoise bear a striking resemblance to similar features of the narrator himself in relation to others and to his writing. Probably the most obvious feature is the obsessive abuse of others to achieve individual goals. Like the kitchen maid whose work and suffering bolster Françoise's sense of well-being as head servant, she, in turn, supports the narrator in his efforts to become a writer. In economic terms, she could be said to constitute part of the material means of the narrator's artistic production. Like the stereotypical housewife in a middle- or working-class household in many parts of the world, the maid in this middle-class home consistently satisfies a variety of physical needs: food and drink, clean clothing, and a clean home. Such satisfaction makes it possible for the narrator to pursue his art. That Françoise's work makes the narrator's art possible is established early in *Combray* in which wholesome dinners refresh the narrator after hours of reading the exploits of his favorite heroes who initiate him into his own adventures as a writer.

Françoise's nurturing of the narrator includes psychological care as well. She is the one in the crucial bedtime scene who acts as intermediary in the eventually successful attempt to have Mamma come to his room. Françoise is also the one who above all others understands the narrator's writing, even if it is only an intuitive sense of his artistic activity. He feels that she admires his work, senses his joy in writing, and that she could be helpful in gluing together the bits of worked-over paper that he produces. A series of identifications occurs in the last section of the novel in which the narrator imagines himself and Françoise working at different jobs side by side in similar ways. His writing is likened to her repairing a dress or a broken kitchen window, and finally, to her cooking a special beef stew (3:1090–91). The description of her stew resonates with Tante Léonie's rich meals themselves suggesting the satisfaction enjoyed in the madeleine scene (see p. 54).

Proust's portrayal of Françoise "represents the common people," to use Bakhtin's phrase, but also reveals the many similarities between master and servant, implicitly criticizes their lives as exploitative and life denying, and dramatizes the hierarchical society of the time. Both the master's and the servant's actions are often described as arbitrary and inflexible, like those of an unjust ruler. In fact Françoise and the narrator are frequently associated with the capriciousness of the primary authority figures of French life: father, priest, and head of state. These associations are prominent from the outset of *Remembrance*, in the bedtime scene in which the servant's code prohibits the delivery of a message to Mamma (1:30), and during the Guermantes Way walk where the narrator confesses that he depends on his father, the government, and God to make of him "the foremost writer" of his time (1:189). Proust reveals how servant and master are equally victimized by social roles in the description of an ultimately self-defeating defense mechanism. Caught inside a hierarchical structure, each tries to reverse the direction of exploitation and succeeds only in reproducing the structure once more. At the beck and call of her masters' bells (2:12; 1:60: the narrator's and Tante Léonie's), Françoise abuses the privilege of ringing for help at Balbec. A different version of her abuse of bell-ringing appears when she categorically refuses to ring for the hot water that her employers occasionally request to warm their feet (1:745–46).

Several early passages in *Remembrance* suggest that Kristeva's concept of a discourse that is at once both symbolic and semiotic illuminates the apparently male Saniette as well as Françoise. That is, Proust's description of the paleographer analyzes the repressive social hierarchies of turn-of-the-century France and also recreates the pleasurable union with the mother. Saniette is shy, simple, and good-natured, and has difficulty pronouncing consonants. For the narrator attempting to enter salon society, Saniette's character, speech, and behavior are those of a child who is incapable of learning the social skills of manhood and who is exploited because of this incompetence. Proust ironically criticizes salon society for abusing Saniette because of his goodness, despite his intelligence, wealth, and aristocratic blood, qualities that normally command respect there:

> . . . Saniette, whose shyness, simplicity and good-nature had lost him most of the consideration he had earned for his skill in palaeography, his large fortune, and the distinguished family to which he belonged. When he spoke, his words came out in a burble which was delightful to hear because one felt that it indicated not so much a defect of speech as a quality of the soul, as if it were a survival from the age of innocence which he had never wholly outgrown. All the consonants which he was unable to pronounce seemed like harsh utterances of which his gentle lips were incapable. (1:221–22)

Within the context of *Remembrance* taken as a whole, Saniette is a character who enables Proust to uncover the power mechanisms of salon society. The brutal scene in which Forcheville reduces the scholar to a stuttering, tearful child in order to impress his new mistress and the Verdurin clan in hopes of becoming a member is a biting satire of social mobility in this milieu. Equally biting is Proust's satire of the master-slave relationship that the Verdurin salon must maintain with Saniette if it is to survive:

> Thanks to his quivering sensibility, his timorous and easily alarmed shyness, Saniette provided them with a whipping-boy for every day in the year. And so, for fear of his defecting, they took care always to invite him with friendly and persuasive words, such as the bigger boys at school or the old soldiers in a regiment address to a greenhorn whom they are anxious to cajole so that they may get him into their clutches with the sole object of ragging and bullying him when he can no longer escape. (2:930–31)

This passage is an example of Proust's use of the notorious images of the French lycée and military to convey the beau monde's cruel hypocrisy. The images make clear the insidious and inevitable way in which both slave and master (Saniette *and* the Verdurins) become dependent on each other.

Proust also uses terms that together suggest the role of the economy in social life—"the value of his wares" and "slips a note"— in the description of Saniette's attempts to be witty (2:901–2). Upper-class French society built on a capitalist framework assigns a monetary function to the individual, even when that individual lacks the assets required of him. The episode reveals the tragedy of Saniette's life: this scene is one of a series in the second half of the novel that dramatizes the evolution in this character from misunderstood scholar to bungling misfit. Caught within social mechanisms that he cannot recognize, let alone control, Saniette becomes more and more the misfit whose melancholy, bitterness, indiscretions, and pedantic language are difficult to bear, even for the formerly sympathetic narrator.

Beyond his more obvious role as a victim whose intellect and charming social naiveté are destroyed by the salon hierarchy, Saniette is, like Françoise, though less developed, a socially marginal character linked in a significant and positive way to the narrator's ability to write. A clue to his centrality appears in Proust's introduction to him, quoted previously. This introduction describes the character and his suffering in salon society. His speech is also a striking metaphor for the madeleine transporting the narrator and the attentive reader to an "original" instant of plenitude.[10] In light of Kristeva's theory, both Saniette's and the narrator's language are examples of a semiotic discourse whispering words that are pronounced differently and that stimulate an oral response. Proust refers to Saniette's speech impediment as a kind of "bouillie" "dans la bouche" [qui] "trahissait une qualité de l'âme," "un reste de l'innocence du premier âge qu'il n'avait jamais perdu . . ." "pabulum" "in the mouth" that "reveals a quality of the soul," "the remains of a childhood innocence that he had never lost . . . ").[11] In the narrator's mouth, the "pabulum"/madeleine arouses the Combray memories that enable him to become a writer.

Reassessing Saniette's and Françoise's roles, I see these apparently minor characters as critical players in Proust's representation of the limits of both fin-de-siècle Symbolist writing and the salon. In the context of Kristeva's theory, *Remembrance* effectively breaks with a society and an aesthetic that derive from French Rationalism, thereby disrupting power relations and liberating the rhythmic life of the psyche and the body. In this broad sense, Proust prepares the terrain for feminism by writing a semiotic discourse recreating the link to the mother.

4

Revisiting Modernism:
DeBeauvoir, Truffaut, and Renoir

DeBeauvoir's *She Came to Stay* (*L'Invitée*, 1943), Truffaut's *Jules and Jim* (*Jules et Jim*, 1962) and Renoir's *The Rules of the Game* (*La Règle du jeu*, 1939) study the problem monogamy posed for many women in mid-twentieth-century France.[1] The examination of three Modernist texts in light of Julia Kristeva's reworking of Freud demonstrates the validity and usefulness of her early theory and lays bare the psychological implications of these works, significant in their own right. The heroine in each work (Françoise, Catherine, and Christine) tries to free herself from monogamy's constraints in an effort to give expression to the physical and emotional life threatened by her relationship to a man. The texts stage three different versions of a struggle to transform a dangerous monogamous relationship.

The social order prevailing in France just before World War II is the cultural context for these artists: an increasingly repressive government under Deladier deriving from Enlightenment philosophy collaborates with the Nazis and produces the Munich accords mentioned in *She Came to Stay*. Middle-class mores, molded early on by French Catholicism and its male God, demand that the woman be monogamous and preferably married, or, more rarely, that she become marginalized, for example, as a courtesan.

From a broad historical perspective, these texts reveal contemporary forms of domination in a period of imperialist regimes in Europe, the United States, and the former Soviet Union, capitalist and socialist both deriving from Enlightenment philosophy, as Zygmunt Bauman explains.[2] The Industrial Revolution, increasing depersonalization, and uniformity contributed to oppressive conditions in many countries during this period. Informed by psychoanalysis, the texts uncover the domination of women and the repression of unconscious desire often associated with the female. Prompted by Kristeva's theory, I examine the gendered patterns of opposition within the female protagonist in DeBeauvoir, Truffaut, and Renoir.

I have selected works that, like Proust's *Remembrance*, resist the hierarchies structuring sexuality in France. Others—Gide's *Immoralist* comes to mind—are also part of a body of texts exploring gendered psychic patterns and constituting a critique of domination. For Kristeva, who has not written on DeBeauvoir, Truffaut, or Renoir at any length, the authority figure underlying the social contract manifested in language is rational and male.[3] She is not speaking of the individuals wielding power in a given society, although they may frequently continue to be male, but rather of the symbolic associations made with them as figures of reason in Western cultures. Freud discussed these associations long ago, for example, in terms of the substitute father of group psychology.[4]

Like Freud, Kristeva recognizes the father's power as expressed by and in language. The Freudian notion of the "father of individual pre-history" underlies her concept of the subject. More generally, she sees language as a substantial influence on the subject and as the primary mode of the subject's existence: it is language that makes the subject knowable. As a result of Jacques Lacan's extensive and influential psychoanalytic theory since the fifties, Kristeva's approach to texts and to patients possesses a legitimacy and context it would not otherwise have. Lacan's concepts of the symbolic order, the name of the father, and the phallus underlie Kristeva's discussion of the speaking subject as a psychic formation that can communicate with others and influence social relations.[5]

While the male is associated with authority and reason, the female is symbolically connected to the physical and the emotional, to pleasure and pain. Kristeva provides support for the existence of these associations by examining the Judeo-Christian tradition in which love is the desire for what a male God forbids. She also demonstrates their validity by referring to Freud's discovery of the memory of symbiosis with the mother. In "Stabat Mater," for instance, pleasure is a reenactment of the union with the mother prior to birth.[6] For Kristeva, it is primarily psychic formations, often including a biological component, that shape social and economic conditions and not the other way around, as for Marx or for the Marxist that Kristeva once was. These formations are expressed in verbal and nonverbal language frequently either positive, rebellious, and pleasure filled, on the one hand, or negative, conforming, and painful, on the other. Kristeva theorizes an alternation between these two languages expressing different psychological orientations. Moving beyond Freud and Lacan and especially the latter's emphasis on the father's role, Kristeva describes an alternation or combination of identifications with father and mother with special emphasis on the latter. She gently shifts the balance of identifications from reason to affect and to the mother with whom it is associated.[7]

For Kristeva, psychoanalytic reading, like the talking cure, reveals the subject lifting the repression that had banished a part of language—the search for the mother—from the public sphere of communication.[8] Such a reading, as in Habermas and Ricoeur, uncovers how the psyche in the text may play a revolutionary role in power relations.

Valorizing affect, the mother, and the semiotic over reason, the father, and the symbolic, Kristeva is able to make the case for language as a source of radical political change while maintaining language's role as communication. The language of her patients and of artists frequently takes the form of a search for the lost object that is the mother, a search marked by depression or, as Kristeva conceives it, abjection. She has shown that abjection manifests itself in violence against others, as in her analysis of Céline's anti-Semitism, or in violence against one's own psyche as in her discussion of allowing authority to repress a part of oneself.[9] Abjection describes the desperate plight of the female protagonists in each of the texts examined here. Yet, for Kristeva, abjection, like other forms of psychological suffering, may ultimately be stimulating and creative.[10]

Kristeva's psychoanalytic theory and criticism are especially useful in examining Modernist texts, as her analyses of the Russian Futurists Khlebnikov and Mayakovsky, Proust, and Céline make clear.[11] Those writing in English and Spanish use the term "Modernist" to refer to literature and film of the period 1860–1960 that reject past and present rational orders. Such texts frequently stage the desire to subvert the social order, a desire that, as this book has been arguing, sustains Kristeva's theory. She has used the term modernity (*modernité*) in a way similar to this use of Modernist to describe twentieth-century texts attempting to cope with the crisis of identity and rationality, a crisis exacerbated by fascism and Stalinism.[12] She has also called attention to woman's role as dissident in such texts.[13] The Modernist sensibility in these texts creates a new kind of politics that is socially and sexually radical in its response to the collaboration with the Nazis in France in the late thirties just before World War II. Women, like minorities, are well positioned because of their history of oppression not only to embody but also to understand the limits of the rational, patriarchal order, as Kristeva and also Henry Adams and Phillip Rieff imply.

For Henry Adams in his *Education,* the Medieval Virgin's sexual and imaginative power shapes early European concepts of woman. A link between generations, she reproduces and gives meaning. Like the Virgin, women are an emblem of power, synthesis, and order, even when the dynamo of the Industrial Revolution in part transforms the feminine, as it does much of modern life, into a monstrous, chaotic entity. The historian, including the historian in each of us, can continue to discover meaningful structure by identifying with a wise and nurturing figure understood as both dynamo and Virgin.

In his insightful analysis of Freud's work, Phillip Rieff also suggests that women are well placed historically and socially to represent and comprehend the boundaries of the rational patriarchal order.

Rieff points out that, for the founder of psychoanalysis, Romantic mythology and fiction describe women as angels or whores, constructed out of both the respectful love originally felt for the mother and genital sexuality.[14] A critique of rational order in politics and the arts, Romanticism is one of the principal influences on Modernism. It is, then, not surprising that Romantic fiction frequently overlaps with Modernist and that a complex female protagonist with characteristics of both the angel and the whore—Flaubert's Madame Bovary is an early example—often embodies a Modernist politics.

In the context of the Modernist text understood in these ways, DeBeauvoir, Truffaut, and Renoir explore a woman's struggle with a male authority figure as she attempts to transform a repressive relationship within a couple. The gendered patterns of opposition prominent in Kristevan theory function in a similar manner in all three works. Her theory leads me to consider each work as a critique of the monogamous female psyche and of the capitalist society that it helps support and that in part sustains it.

A review of the criticism on *Jules and Jim* reveals that, although critics have not seen its similarities to *She Came to Stay*, certain critics such as James Monaco, Roger Greenspun, and David Davidson suggest a rapport between the film and the novel, a link based on an existential context and on a male/female opposition. Monaco and Greenspun along with Allen Thiher discuss the existential framework underlying the film. In his book *The New Wave*, Monaco demonstrates the dramatic tension between Catherine's existence and the images and symbols that Jules and Jim try to impose on her.[15] In Sartrean terms, the *pour-soi* that is Catherine's consciousness struggles with the *en-soi* that men invariably construct for her.

Greenspun's epigraph also alludes to the existential framework that links Truffaut to DeBeauvoir.[16] The quotation from Goethe's *Elective Affinities*, the book that Catherine borrows from Jules, states, "Life to them was a rat's hell—they could flee it only with each other." The line appears to contradict the Sartrean notion that "hell is other people." Common to both quotations is the idea that an individual's existence, whether heaven or hell, is necessarily an existence *in the world*, inevitably a product tied to the lives of others—in Kristeva's framework, to both conscious and unconscious formations of male and female.

Davidson's commentary points directly to the conflict-ridden protagonist common in both film and novel and, in fact, while he does not discuss *She Came to Stay*, he makes use of DeBeauvoir in describing women's double bind.[17] His comparative study of G. W. Pabst's *Pandora's Box*, Josef Von Sternberg's *The Blue Angel*, and Truffaut's *Jules and Jim* outlines the masculine, European, and Modernist sensibility that creates a new kind of moral female character who is a sexual and social libertarian. Davidson borrows from *The Second Sex* DeBeauvoir's definition of the contradiction that often creates a double bind for women, at least in the West. He applies this definition to the female character he is describing: on the one hand, she "belongs to man" and serves a variety of social needs; on the other hand, she remains "foreign to man," and violates morality and social conventions.

Thus, readings of *She Came to Stay* and *Jules and Jim* from the sixties through the eighties, often written in an existential frame, call attention to the gendered patterns that Kristeva's theory examines. Francis Jeanson's seminal study of DeBeauvoir's life and work analyzes a fundamental opposition between, on the one hand, the notion of contingency represented by the concrete femininity of maternal flesh and, on the other hand, the notion of transcendence, conveyed by the abstract virility of paternal consciousness.[18] Though Jeanson rejects a psychoanalytic reading, his opposition between contingency and transcendence resembles the female and male identifications that characterize Françoise (and Catherine) from a Kristevan perspective.

One of the finest analyses of *She Came to Stay* appears in Maurice Merleau-Ponty's *Sense and Non-sense* in which he digresses for a second from his phenomenological reading to point out a parallel between the public and private spheres in the novel.[19] Claiming to be generous, like imperialistic France in its dealings with other countries according to the so-called universalistic policies of the National Convention beginning in 1792, Pierre and Françoise exercise their mastery and verify the universality of their lives in their relationship with each other and with other people. For Merleau-Ponty who does not speak of sexual difference or patriarchy, the state, the couple, and the individual function according to a similar psychological and political model. Kristeva's theory helps identify and reveal the function of this model as the rationalist patriarchal paradigm in DeBeauvoir, Truffaut, and Renoir. In *She Came to Stay*, the paradigm underlies the French intellectual—Françoise and Pierre both individually and as a couple, Merleau-Ponty implies. DeBeauvoir and Sartre themselves corroborate this model.

While it appears in the narratives that patriarchal structures are biologically grounded, that is, embodied in actual men, the texts (including Davidson's essay), read against Kristeva's theory, show that the link between authority and the male is psychologically constructed and not necessarily biological. At the same time, there is a biological component in Kristeva's neo-Freudian analysis: symbiosis with the mother establishes the first link to gendered experience—the link between physical well-being and the female. As the child acquires language in the process of becoming socialized, a second link is forged that complements the first and is psychological, the link between authority and the male, deriving at least in part from the Judeo-Christian tradition.

She Came to Stay was published in 1943, some nineteen years before the appearance of *Jules and Jim*. The novel tells the story of Françoise's life in 1939 during the German occupation of France with emphasis on her attempt to free herself from the limits of a monogamous relationship. She struggles to express her ideas, emotions, and sensations in writing and, most important, in living with her lover Pierre and close friends Xavière and Gerbert. From the beginning of the novel in which she initially decides not to pursue Gerbert whom she clearly desires, Françoise's love for Pierre is revealed as something different from the perfect union she thinks it is: "We are simply one." Despite her claims that the relationship is a reciprocal, egalitarian one in which each member participates fully, this is not the case. A double standard contains her sexual activity within her relationship to Pierre. The language she uses in discussing the subject with him suggests repression: "But I wouldn't be interested in an affair which had no continuity. . . . No . . I can't help myself: I'm the faithful type . . . [and to herself] we are simply one" (25–26). Her words imply a partly involuntary submission of herself as female subject to the virile entity that Pierre represents. This submission is emphasized in the last sentence, a repetition of Pierre's preceding words.

Françoise's actions reveal that she unwittingly stifles her sexuality and emotions in her life with Pierre. He functions as a male censor who must approve her acts, including the act of writing that could establish an identity for her. Early on in *She Came to Stay*, after just completing a scene in the novel she is writing, her immediate reaction is, "There. Let's hope he likes this. I think it'll please him" (DeBeauvoir, 18). Restrictive phrases (like the "pourvu que" ["if only"] in the original of this line [DeBeauvoir, 19]) dominate in her speech and thoughts in the later scene with Pierre and indicate a pattern of behavior. Françoise, at least until the novel's conclusion, subordinates other activities to her love for Pierre and this love, as we have seen, subordinates her desires to his: "The *only* something new which interests me is our future together. I can't help it. That's what makes me happy. You've *no one* to blame *but* yourself" (DeBeauvoir, 25; emphasis added).

In an early scene describing her relationship with Xavière just prior to the formation of the trio, Françoise attempts to live an existence that she must repress in her life with Pierre:

> But what was especially wonderful was her having attached this pathetic little being to her own life. For . . . Xavière now belonged to her. Nothing ever gave Françoise more intense joy than this kind of possession.
>
> Xavière was absorbed in the dancing girl. She could not see her own face, its beauty heightened by emotion. Her fingers stroked the contours of the cup which she was holding lightly in her hand, but Françoise alone was aware of the contours of that hand. Xavière's gestures, her face, her very life depended on Françoise for their existence . . . for Françoise, Xavière's childhood, her days of stagnation, her distastes were a

romantic story as real as the delicate contour of her cheeks. And it was right here in this café, among the varicolored hangings, that the story ended, this precise moment in Françoise's life when she turned to look at Xavière and study her. (DeBeauvoir, 20)

Joy, beauty, a sense of being needed, a linguistic quality ("a romantic story"), curved, female shapes ("the cup," "that hand," and "her cheeks"), these characteristics suggest an experience that in many ways reverses the repression visible in the earlier passages. No longer submitting herself as female to a male censor, she seems to unite with a female figure that enables her to live more fully, as does Xavière in watching the dancing girls. Here, Françoise does not repeat the inaccurate words of a male authority figure as at the end of the conversation about her faithfulness, but translates the stuff of Xavière's existence into an exhilarating novel that becomes a precious moment in Françoise's own life. While Xavière is a woman, it is not biological necessity that creates the precious moment but rather a psychic formation that is gendered as Kristeva's theory helps make clear. De-Beauvoir herself writes in *The Second Sex* the well-known words, "One is not born a woman, but becomes one." In the passage on Xavière, the curved shapes resemble certain actual female contours, but are primarily images that Françoise assembles in a construction of "the female" within Western culture. Xavière's dependent personality, perceived by Françoise in the quoted passage, is part of that construction, another component in her "romantic story." This story, unfortunately, is short-lived in the life of the trio—more frequent as the novel progresses are moments of jealousy and particularly of alienation and repression as it becomes obvious that life with Xavière and Pierre is more painful and stifling than life with Pierre alone. Not unlike a mother and wife, Françoise increasingly comes to compete with Pierre as the figure of authority in a triangular relationship. She is thus at the same time reproducing the model she is attempting to transform. In Toril Moi's psychoanalytic reading, the alienated Françoise is more like a daughter who has idealized the father (Pierre) she desires, hates the one who is the father's primary love object, the mother (Xavière), and is unable to progress to a mature identification with her.[20] Whether "mother/wife" or "daughter," a seriously troubled Françoise is coping with a threatening male.

One scene in particular is effective in conveying Françoise's alienation. She is seated on the terrace of the Café Deux Magots and remembers a childhood episode without seeing any connection between the memory and her current depression. At six years of age, she finds herself alone one day on the second floor landing of her home, studying an old jacket hanging on the back of a chair. What captures her attention is the jacket's lack of consciousness, its inability to express what it is, compared to her own ability as a human to do so. It is no coincidence that a parallel is drawn between this object from her childhood and the jealous, alienated, and perplexed writer who is no more able to articulate the connection between past and present than to give expression to the repressed desire within her.

Life within the trio is not the positive, dynamic experience it had at first promised to be. In the conclusion, after Xavière too had begun to care for Gerbert, Françoise kills Xavière to destroy the anguish caused by Xavière's partially correct perception that Françoise betrayed her friendship by sleeping with Gerbert. In light of Kristeva's theory, Françoise has been trying to reconcile the demands of desire and reason tearing her apart to find a balance enabling her to live more fully. The murder stages the tragic conclusion. Killing Xavière, Françoise attempts to satisfy her emotional and sexual need for Gerbert and Pierre and rejects the authority figure outside and within herself. She violates French law literally and also figuratively in the sense that she does not obey middle-class mores requiring her to be at least monogamous if not married. More important, Françoise's final description of the murder—I return to this in my conclusion—indicates that, while liberating her momentarily from the anguish of Xavière's judgment of her, it is ultimately a form of oppression in which she seeks to exercise absolute authority.

At first glance, Truffaut's Catherine seems more similar to Xavière than to DeBeauvoir's Françoise. Emotional, willful, attractive, intelligent, for the most part unattached to any project or individual, this description could apply to either woman. Like Xavière,

Catherine is far less generous and lucid vis-à-vis other people than is Françoise. Yet, Xavière, on the one hand, seems to have rejected authority figures early on or to have been overcome by such a figure before a battle could begin. Catherine, on the other hand, is struggling as fiercely as Françoise with an internalized male

Catherine's story starts by cutting her out. Truffaut's portrayal of his heroine begins with a title naming only the two male protagonists, *Jules and Jim*, and with a cluster of stereotypes—she is sphinx, passive woman, and horrified spectator. The screen remains dark for a few seconds as Catherine mysteriously declares, as if to a lover, "You said to me: I love you. I said to you: wait. I was going to say: take me. You said to me: go away."[21] The words suggest that Catherine plays the role of the passive woman, as she appears to consent to the male authority dictating her life. Truffaut reveals a conflicted psyche in the distance she experiences from herself in this opening scene where Catherine, who is normally presented from a male perspective, Jules' and Jim's, as many critics have noticed, is presented directly in the voice-over. As the quotation reveals, the male initiates, interrupts, and terminates the love affairs that comprise her life. The alienated and horrified female psyche, present in the voice-over for the appropriately blank screen, comments on the drama suppressing her own drives and rhythms.

Evidence of the internalized authority figure appears once again about halfway through the film when Jules and Catherine reveal to Jim that she is severely depressed. The different versions they give of the problem conclude that Catherine experiences marriage as a prison where she is dismayed to find herself no longer free but forced to confront a man to whom she is bound: "there we were, face to face, linked together" (72). She explains that in the end she had to tell Jules, "I am taking back my liberty" (59). Catherine internalizes a male figure to such an extent that because of its tyranny she is drawn back to Jules after breaking free of him for six months. This internalization grows even stronger when she exchanges the unaggressive, tolerant Jules for the more demanding Jim who becomes her lover, and who, ironically enough, demands that she remain faithful by not sleeping with her husband.

Kristeva's view of the individual as a complex web of desire and reason frequently in conflict helps explain an aspect of the film that is otherwise difficult to analyze. Why does the Catherine who comes to resist domesticity insist on having a second child in the last half of the film, rejecting Jim when she miscarries? For Kristeva, having a child can be a way of reviving desire and of living creatively. Reversing the mother/baby roles and without sacrificing her own personality, a woman revives the early experience of symbiotic pleasure enjoyed with her own mother as well as of later episodes of physical union with others. Becoming a mother also has the potential to legitimize sexuality, to give that desire a symbolic existence to the extent that the child functions as a symbol of domesticated desire in Western cultures, as Freud recognized.[22] The episodes in which Catherine and Jules's daughter, Sabine, relax with the trio (rolling in the fields, playing the village idiots' game, listening to the love song performed by Catherine and Albert who has now become one of her lovers) suggests that the little girl functions for a time in this way. The playful episodes come to an end as Catherine increasingly struggles and submits to an internalized male figure. The child then comes to represent primarily submission to authority. Catherine must not only marry a man and be faithful to him but also raise his child.

Like Françoise who, for a while at least, creates precious moments by incorporating Xavière into her life with Pierre and, in the end, by killing her, Catherine initially creates such moments by becoming Jim's lover while at the same time maintaining a close relationship to Jules. The climax of the film occurs once Catherine and Jim are lovers. While Truffaut is among the most verbal of filmmakers and narrates through dialogue and voice-over, he also tells Catherine's story by manipulating the sequences of images and music that constitute part of the specificity of his medium. Here, Delerue's score makes an abrupt change in the sound track, conveying the fragility and joy of this ménage à trois. Slow, solemn music (and less often, a few ominous notes) suddenly becomes lyrical, playful, and upbeat wind instruments and violins, with the stylized repetitions associated with nursery rhymes. Panning shots link ill-fated scenes on the terrace and in the German countryside to the short-lived adventures the trio had enjoyed in Paris and on the southern coast of France. Music and panning combine with the characters' body language (biking, running, swinging from trees, swimming, sunbathing, rolling over in the grass, singing, playing the game of the village idiot) in both parts of the film to create the fluid movements of sensual adventures as Catherine briefly escapes from depression understood as abject submission to a tyrant incorporated within herself. The adventures can be seen as a mise-en-scène of the return to the mother à la Kristeva with Catherine as both a nurturing figure and lovely schoolgirl, images that together depict mother and child. No longer the monogamous woman, Catherine enjoys being with Jules and Jim, joined from time to time by Sabine and Albert. Truffaut shoots the scenes in such a way that Catherine is at the center and often takes the lead, not controlling the others, but enabling them to find pleasure that is at once physical, aesthetic, and life giving.

Viewed against Kristeva's theory, Truffaut's film conveys Catherine's attempt to transform a stifling monogamous relationship with Jules into a freer, more positive one with Jules and Jim. Truffaut projects a sequence of images revealing first Jules and Jim's friendship, their pursuit of women, then Catherine's relationships with them. Their relationship with Catherine begins as a quest for a beautiful object. Albert, initially Jules's acquaintance befriends promising artists and shares his slide photographs of art depicting beautiful women with Jules and Jim. The most significant of the slides is that of the excavated statue with the fascinating smile. The two friends discover that smile on Catherine's face when Albert introduces her to them.

Early episodes such as the ones involving Albert show a relentless reification of women and Catherine's struggle via fire and water to destroy herself as sexual object. Instances of her efforts to destroy herself from the first half of the film include her burning of old love letters that she calls "lies" and her rejection of Baudelaire's definition of woman as "natural, therefore abominable." Within the total sequence of images that makes up the film as I have described it, these examples can be seen as attempts to get rid of an oppressive phallic presence within herself. In the first example, Catherine comes close to setting herself on fire as she destroys the vestiges of a love affair that was a deceitful and painful rejection. In the second, she risks drowning by jumping into the Seine to cut off a painful discussion of sexist conceptions of what it means to be female and to take revenge on Jules by scaring him. The concluding scenes show Catherine wearing a man's tie, wire-rimmed glasses, and a cloche covering her long wavy hair. She says and moves little, evoking rigidity and a lack of freedom, energy, and spirit. In the context of the rest of the film and of Kristeva's theory, she gives in to that part of herself demanding submission and censoring pleasure. Catherine is then drowned along with Jim when she deliberately drives over a half-destroyed bridge into the Seine.

Kristeva's theory of psychic formation in the West helps uncover a different version of the troubled monogamous woman in Renoir's *Rules of the Game*. It is a well-known fact that Renoir has exerted considerable influence on Truffaut who writes that "the work of Jean Renoir is the work of an infallible film maker [sic]," "Renoir has succeeded in creating the most alive films in the history of the cinema."[23] That Renoir has recognized parallels in his work and Truffaut's is perhaps less well-known.[24] A critique of French society (Renoir's movie includes the irony of the disclaimer necessitated by the fear of state censorship that it is not meant as social criticism [*étude de moeurs*]), marital versus extramarital love, friendship, and the German character as natural and spontaneous are prominent in both *Rules of the Game* and *Jules and Jim*. A more fundamental similarity can be found in the way both films examine the male/female oppositions that create conflict in an anxiety-ridden female psyche. While it is not part of this chapter, the inclusion of many significant same-sex relations in the DeBeauvoir, Truffaut, and Renoir texts examined here is noteworthy in the context of a homophobic France.[25]

A few critics have suggested the central role women play in these films; none, to my knowledge, mention the thematic and structural similarities in *Rules of the Game* and *Jules and Jim*. In an essay that deals primarily with the sound track as a fundamental structuring element, Michael Little discusses Renoir's creation of female characters who are nonconformists.[26] Little convincingly argues that music is frequently used to juxtapose scenes in which husbands strike a powerful pose (Robert showing off his mechanical] organ in the ballroom, Schumacher praising his native Alsace in the kitchen) with scenes in which their wives are redefining their sexual roles outside of marriage (Christine with André, Octave, and Saint Aubin; Lisette with Marceau).

Nick Browne reads *Rules of the Game* as a critique of capitalist society and of its denial of the individual's sexuality.[27] His study of Robert's and Schumacher's erotic property relations toward their wives emphasizes the women's paucity of affection for their husbands, figures of authority more than of love. Browne's analysis is particularly valuable in that it shows how Renoir films Christine's relations with both her husband and her best friend. After describing the early scene in which Christine laughs with Octave and pushes him down on her bed as an instance of extramarital erotic play, Browne gives a subtle analysis of Renoir's use of the camera in photographing the scene. Robert's entrance into the bedroom is filmed at a different angle than Octave's to show that unlike his wife's friend, he must cross a threshold and ask permission to enter. Renoir is underlining the formal, theatrical role of the husband as the representative of authority not visible in Christine's relationships with Octave and André.

Browne also recognizes that Christine plays a central role in the film, though he does not describe her role at any length. He declares that, as a naive foreigner, she is often distinguished from the other characters and identified with Renoir as represented in the overall structure of his film. Christine's complex psychology, the internal conflict between the authority figure she has interiorized and the desire for love and affection, remains to be explicated. More recently, Julia Lesage uses a structuralist approach based on Roland Barthes's *S/Z* to suggest that Christine's conflict reproduces the sexual and economic relationships that penetrate society.[28] Kristeva's work argues that it is the other way around: sexual and economic relationships reproduce psychological structures. Having rejected structuralism

precisely because of its rationalism and failure to recognize the subject's autonomy, partial though it may be, Kristeva stresses the
importance of character as a psyche shaping social relations.

Christine's attempts to reshape her relationships to her husband, Robert, her lover, André, and her friend, Octave, drive the
plot of *Rules of the Game.* Renoir himself identifies the central role
Christine plays when he says, "But what I want people to feel in this
film is my great love for women. To do this I must show men . . . my
heroine will be Christine."[29] He immediately juxtaposes the main
elements in Christine's conflict. The epigraph from Beaumarchais
valorizes her "changing love." The opening scene introduces the
dashing, courageous aviator, André, whose disappointment at not
finding Christine upon his arrival at Le Bourget airport is evident.
In the following scene in which she talks with Lisette and Robert
about marital happiness and "the natural," a pensive Christine begins to question her marriage as a source of happiness and to consider whether she loves Robert and whether she could live a more
satisfying life with André. At the same time, she recognizes the need
for a degree of social approval and accepts wearing a violet lipstick
as part of her role as Robert's wife, for example.

The interweaving of action, images, and dialogue reveals that
male authority, one of the meanings of the film's title, *La règle du
jeu,* as I read it, represses Christine from within. In Renoir, both rebellion and conformity are fraught with danger: rebellion—leaving
Robert—would probably result in abandonment by André whose
stalling reveals he is not yet ready to go off with her. Conformity is
equally dangerous. Staying with Robert in the ending signals the
failure of her attempt to find a measure of happiness. Kristeva's theory indicates and helps one understand what Renoir's film suggests:
a fragile alternation between rebellion and conformity is required
for the woman to find the appropriate "language" in which to live.

From the beginning, Christine plays a predominantly male-
oriented role. Like Catherine in *Jules et Jim,* she is often seen from
the perspective of the men who love her as in the opening when she
is described by André as the inspiration for his historic transatlantic
flight. When she does appear on the screen, her German accent

suggests that she is a misfit who plays a role that is as foreign to her as French. The camera often focuses on her as the companion who attends beau monde soirées on her husband's arm and entertains in their chateau, La Colinière. Although it is desire for the aviator that leads her to agree to invite André to the chateau, she seeks the relationship at least in part to punish Robert for his infidelity. Her discovery through the field glasses of Robert embracing Geneviève during the hunt scene proves to be a decisive moment: for a time, Christine pursues André and rejects the role of wife more forcefully. Finally, without André's or Octave's support, she retreats back into her marriage and gives up the attempt to free herself. She sees that André, like many others, will allow himself to become a puppet much like those used in the evocative *Danse macabre* during the weekend festivities at La Colinière. Instead of cutting the strings of convention and helping Christine, he wants time to tell Robert that he and Christine plan to leave together and suggests that she stay with his mother. Christine sees that Octave, too, lacks the energy and drive necessary to run off with her and consequently she feels compelled to conform and returns to Robert.

Her dialogue, in conjunction with behavior that does not take the initiative but rather responds to the initiative of the men around her, reveals an intuitive sense of the authority figure she has internalized. The early comment to Lisette, "Oh well, what is natural nowadays," like the later comments to Robert and Jackie respectively, "A lie is a very heavy garment to carry around" and "People are looking at you," conveys her alienation as wife and points to a foreign presence as the source of her malaise. More than once Renoir uses the image of the garment as a male presence that imposes itself on the woman. Just after Christine uses the image to describe the lie Robert understands in terms of André but that actually refers to her marriage, she appears in the white coat her husband purchased for her to accompany him to social engagements. Later she will put on Lisette's cape, a garment disliked by the maid who received it from her husband, Schumacher.

The cape is one of the elements that link Christine to Lisette and to the psychic formations characterizing them and their society.

Renoir uses the servants as he does the beau monde (the hunt along with the mechanical dolls and organ collected by Robert) to reveal the dominating presence in French life. As the scenes are projected on the screen in a series of increasingly mobile images, the male authority figure emerges: Schumacher and Corneille among the servants, Robert among the wealthy and among his collection of mechanical objects. This figure then loses control in the climactic scenes in which the organ emits a deafening roar and Schumacher unsuccessfully tries to shoot Marceau who has been pursuing Lisette. Finally, the figure reasserts itself as a weakened presence in the ending of the film as Robert offers his unconvincing explanation of André's death. He states that Schumacher was trying to catch a poacher. In fact, the servant was intending to kill Octave whom he mistakenly believed to be pursuing Lisette. André had been attempting to run away with Christine once Octave became convinced that he himself could not make her happy. After his explanation, Robert guides everyone back into his chateau amid the sinister shadows of the cypress trees.

The final scene also makes a connection between the death of the individual and the death of the nation. After its first showing in 1939, the film was accurately perceived as Renoir's critique of France's collaboration with Germany in the signing of the Munich accords and was initially banned. That Robert is Jewish is an instance of the ironic subtleties of this critique.

Robin Bates's psychoanalytic reading of *Rules of the Game* studies the connection between the personal and the political by focusing on the male figures. He sees *Rules of the Game* as a film revealing the violence about to erupt in France in the late thirties, violence deriving from gender tensions in crisis. For him, the movie portrays France anxious about its lack of male leaders in a Europe dominated by Hitler, Mussolini, and Franco. *Rules of the Game* portrays male posturing and calls for an uncovering of male fears and confronting the consequences of failure.[30] More to the point of the film as a whole and in the context of this book, Renoir depicts France as a country in which the assertion of male authority leads to tragedy both for its women and Europe in 1939.

A tragic twist occurs in the ending of the three works I examine here. In *Rules of the Game*, the attempt to topple a weakened authority is prematurely aborted when André is accidentally killed. In *She Came to Stay* and *Jules and Jim*, the repressed drive that struggles unsuccessfully against the male manifests itself in a violent act that reproduces the very model it is attempting to destroy Françoise's murder of Xavière no less than Catherine's murder of Jim and herself is ultimately another form of oppression.

Françoise, seen by a narrator who often unites with her in indirect discourse, possesses the traits of a despotic ruler who has ordered an execution, a ruler who is not unlike the male authority figure she has been fighting: "Alone. She had acted alone. . . . No one could condemn or absolve her. Her act was her very own. *I have done it of my own free will.* It was her own will which was being fulfilled, now nothing separated her from herself. She had chosen at last. She had chosen herself" (DeBeauvoir, 404). Whereas Françoise, who is usually, and by far, the more lucid of the two heroines, deludes herself in the conclusion, believing she can act with godlike impunity, Catherine does not. Killing herself in the same act that kills Jim, in the throes of a kind of abjection that Kristeva has described at some length, she may sense what Truffaut and DeBeauvoir reveal. Using power to harm others is not unlike allowing authority to repress a part of yourself.

Neither an aborted attempt to forge a relationship outside of marriage nor violent acts that reproduce aggression could be considered an adequate solution to the problem of the psychic formations defining power and society in France. Without providing solutions, DeBeauvoir, Truffaut, and Renoir transform psychological pain into thought-provoking texts signaling significant changes in French sensibility, like the "smoke rising from the chimney-stacks" that José Ortega y Gasset described in what was one of the first discussions of Modernism in 1925.[31] Considered together from the perspective of Julia Kristeva's work, *She Came to Stay*, *Jules and Jim*, and *Rules of the Game* examine gendered psychic structures and acknowledge their tragic consequences in mid-twentieth-century France.

❦ 5 ❧

The Two Faces of the Mother's Mask: Céline and China

Kristeva's political position becomes more clearly defined in her writing on Céline and China.[1] In *Powers of Horror: An Essay on Abjection* (*Pouvoirs de l'horreur: Essai sur l'abjection*, 1980), *About Chinese Women*, (*Des Chinoises*, 1974), and *The Samurai* (*Les Samuraï*, 1991), she analyzes both Céline's work and China in positive terms, while indicating the dangers lurking in each. Confronting prohibition and repression, Kristeva's psychoanalytic writing takes on two controversial subjects whose ideologies have been rightfully condemned: Céline for his anti-Semitic political pamphlets and China for authoritarian government.

An examination of Kristeva's probing discussion of the other in these three works reflects the developments in her thinking during the period 1974-91. Her version of feminism in these years, despite her criticism of some feminists, coincides with critical events in her biography and an increasing interest in China and in Jews. During this period when she wrote several of her most influential books including the three discussed in this chapter, she married Philippe Sollers, the editor of the well-known journal *Tel Quel*; took a long trip to China; had a child; became a professor at both the University of Paris and Columbia University; began her psychoanalytic practice; and developed close friendships with the novelist Philip Roth and the philosopher Bernard Lévy. Like that of Olga, one of the protagonists in *The Samurai*, Kristeva's feminist perspective is marked by nuance. The figure of the mother emerging in apparently very different texts written over many years creates a complex dialectic in these volumes and throughout her work. Like Lacan, Kristeva's understanding of the mother as a source of both pleasure and pain enables her to theorize a gender-inflected language not determined primarily by biology. In these works, she analyzes the associations Western cultures make with the female and calls attention to a sexism that is foundational and that will resurface in Freud's and Lacan's theories. While she has criticized the work of some feminists in, for example, *Tales of Love* (374), Kristeva's status and stature as a feminist psychoanalytic writer is clear in *Powers of Horror*, *About Chinese Women*, and *The Samurai*. In these texts she speaks more concretely about two oppressed groups, women and Jews, and in *Powers of Horror*, about the relation between them.

The focus of this chapter is her theory of the other, the mother, and the Jew in Céline and in Communist China in 1974. For Kristeva, the writer needs to embrace an identity that is not his or her own in an effort to understand and reveal the ways in which threatening, patriarchal psychic structures shaped personal and public life in early twentieth-century France and more generally in the West. Given that patriarchal society is built on a psychic formation that is unitary, rational, and male, the individual succeeds in changing that psychic structure by identifying with the female.

Kristeva's theory of abjection, part of a broad study of Western culture, takes shape slowly in the spare complex prose of *Powers of Horror*. The first section of *Powers* clarifies the term "abjection" and, in so doing, describes the first years of life when the need for masking emerges. In its broadest sense, "abjection" is the simultaneous attraction and repulsion for the body that derives from the moment when the child's symbiosis with the mother is interrupted. During those early years, the child comes to recognize the father's authority underlying the social contract, the bond enabling one to learn a language, and separates from the mother and the "impure" bodily experience that she represents. For these reasons, according to Kristeva, later identifications with the mother are a mixed blessing. Along with the pleasurable possibility of replaying an earlier symbiosis, confronting and identifying with the mother threatens the individual's relationship to patriarchal authority and brings on feelings of abjection. Confronting the mother at later stages often means transforming one's identity, in particular, yielding one's social presence and sense of self, and experiencing acute depression.

In the next section on forms of abjection in Judeo-Christian religions, *Powers of Horror* demonstrates how desire for the mother and identification with her oppose the religious belief that such desire is impure, a transgression against the male God and the society built on his authority. Kristeva concentrates on those episodes in the history of the West when a recognition of the mother's worth emerges in the very instant she is most strongly rejected. She shows, for example, how Judaism links menstrual blood and excrement to the mother and considers contact with these substances a defilement. The intricate purification rituals of Judaism indirectly reveal the weakness of its official values. The condemnation of the mother apparent in these rites, in fact, testifies to her strength as a threat to the social order and to its values.

Within a global discussion of practices that associate woman with impurity, Kristeva pinpoints the ways in which Judeo-Christian traditions rely on the murder and incest taboos in order to exist. Bringing her neo-Freudian theory to bear on early Jewish history and the ways in which it exemplifies the Oedipal complex (murder of the father/union with the mother), she shows that the prohibition against murder and incest are two sides of the coin that dominates this epoch. The murder and incest taboos are linked in that both grow out of the child's ambivalent relationship to the parents as language is acquired.

In an attempt to protect themselves from murder, the Jewish people replace the killing of the father reenacted in sacrificial rites with the incest taboo. This taboo multiplies in the increasing number of distinctions between "pure" and "impure" while the murder taboo becomes less obvious and the practice of sacrifice dies out. As the role of the incest taboo expands, Judeo-Christian tradition increasingly locates the impure within the subject. Consequently, the Jews grow increasingly guilt ridden. In Kristeva's version of Catholicism's birth, a significant part of the legacy of Judaism as it appears in the New Testament and in Catholic ritual is the ambivalent concept of the body connecting love and sin, that is, the body as both an abject source of illicit drives and a spiritual vessel infused with divine speech (Luke 7). Her rereading of the Bible, including the Old and New Testaments, is impressive in both its detail and cohesiveness: she discusses food taboos, corporeal alteration and death, as well as the woman's body and incest, for example. Her analysis of the logical system of oppositions demonstrating conformity to the law and the discussion of the taboo against the mother as the originating Biblical mytheme (105) sheds new light on a text long considered familiar. In Holy Communion, the sinner finds relief from guilt in confession and the Eucharist while at the same time remaining a "heterogeneous" subject, marked by the early union with the archaic, pleasure-giving mother. The connection between sin and love persists in the West for generations to follow as Kristeva makes clear in her later book on Proust and in her analysis of Céline.

In the third part of *Powers*, Kristeva's theory of abjection becomes more concrete and compelling as she focuses her discussion of "the West" and "Judeo-Christian practices" on Céline's writing. Here and in the other books, her best theoretical writing takes on a specific human face. For Kristeva, Céline, whose courage and insight she first discussed in *Polylogue* in 1973, uncovers the decay in modern patriarchal life while affirming its material base. He creates metaphors that "cover" everyday life in order to better reveal its "social disease" or its possibilities of pleasure. One example is the metaphor of darkness: in Céline's novel *Journey to the End of the Night*, darkness blackens the title and nearly every major episode of the confession of its first-person narrator Ferdinand.[2] Another example is the metaphor of the mother's face that Ferdinand uses from time to time to mask his own in an attempt to transform an identity that society considers inadequately virile: if society rejects his kind of "manhood," then he will adopt womanhood and what the public considers the face of abjection.

Journey to the End of the Night is the tragic–comic confession of a middle-aged physician who has always felt himself to be an outsider and who has suffered from war, poverty, and acute depression, relieved only rarely by glimmers of affection and generosity. In Kristeva's reading of this classic, Céline constructs and deconstructs an inexorably reasonable world in which reason is primarily the marketplace that demands that one become self-seeking and aloof. The author, understood in the overall structure of his novel, is both enemy and accomplice of the society that makes Ferdinand suffer.

Céline's ambivalent relationship to the social contract makes itself manifest in the creation of the alienated Ferdinand and of his alter ego, Léon Robinson. While Robinson appears to reject society by flouting convention and the law, he in fact supplies the values that, by complying with the marketplace's demands that one become independent of others and self-seeking, sustain the market and permeate the world of *Voyage to the End of the Night*.[3]

Those characters who manage to resist the demand that you become self-seeking play a marginal role in the world: Molly, the prostitute whom Ferdinand loves but not enough to stay with her and allow her to change him, and Bébert, the child whose engaging grin is doomed to disappear with age until he dies of typhoid fever before he is allowed to grow up. Women and children like Molly and Bébert, and "unmanly" men, like Ferdinand, live on the fringes of an economy dominated by "virile men" and visited occasionally by egotists like Robinson. Céline indicts this economy with subtlety and force by showing that it is afraid to call itself into question, to change, to "confront the female" in Kristeva's terms.

Her analysis seems to be a loosely organized discussion of his writing viewed as a whole with all its intertextual references. The discussion is, in fact, tightly organized around three principal notions: (1) the confrontation and identification with the mother in the course of Ferdinand's carnivalesque voyage in *Journey to the End of the Night*, (2) the form of the novel: the use of rhythmic patterns to deconstruct syntactic conventions and to convey union with the mother, and (3) the Jew: the anti-Semitism of Céline's political pamphlets gives way to an ambivalent fascination with the figure of the

Jew in the novels. Like the mother, a problematic figure in Kristeva's theory and criticism, he is at one and the same time victim
and threat for the writer.

Ferdinand confronts the mother in the course of his carnivalesque voyage to the end of the night. A masked woman appears in
the confrontation and identification Kristeva describes, as in this
passage from her chapter entitled "Those Females Who Can Wreck
the Infinite":

> Giving life—snatching life away: the Célinian mother
> is Janus-faced, she married beauty and death. She is a con-
> dition of writing, for life given without infinity aspires to
> find its supplement of lacework within words; she is also
> the black power who points to the ephemeral nature of
> sublimation and the unrelenting end of life, the death of
> man. The paranoid woman, another Célinian character, is
> perhaps a projection of the danger of death prompted
> within the speaking being by his perception of that part of
> himself he fantasies as maternal and feminine. (161)

Defining woman as a powerless, impure body, patriarchy produces a female figure who simultaneously (1) offers life—she is the
source of the writer's desires—and (2) who threatens him or her
with death—she represents a life that is mortal. This Janus-faced figure of the mother appears throughout *Journey to the End of the Night*.
On the one hand, there is the prostitute Molly, the woman who
gives life, who arouses admiration and affection in Ferdinand. On
the other hand, there is his mother and the two Henrouilles
(mother and daughter-in-law) who take life away. Ferdinand's
mother directs the death drive inward toward herself and is constantly depressed: the two Henrouilles direct the death drive out-
ward and are relentlessly aggressive and violent.

Céline situates his confrontation with the figure of the mother
in the narrator, Ferdinand. The author took his own mother's name,
Céline, as his pseudonym. Her job was to repair lacework, a fact to
which Kristeva alludes in the passage above. The creation of a first-

person narrator who sometimes coincides with Céline himself is one of the ways he uses the form of the novel to enact an identification with the figures of mother and woman. The irony that Kristeva points out—a kind of irony often present in good fiction—is that Céline confronts the figure of woman precisely at the very moment that his narrator is afraid of doing so. Ferdinand needs to keep Molly at a distance not only figuratively but also literally by transforming her into an ideal (as Céline himself frequently idealizes in creating his most attractive female characters): he abandons her in the United States to avoid all physical contact and the threat that sexual desire represents.

A second way in which Céline enacts an identification with the mother is the use of rhythmic patterns to deconstruct syntactic conventions. Building on Leo Spitzer's work, Kristeva highlights Céline's unusual syntax, indicating its similarities to speech that is outside of the Western mainstream (children's, colloquial, Hungarian, classical Chinese). She shows how Céline's unconventional syntax, along with his use of other devices (first-person narration and ellipsis) creates a language whose logic is more psychological than rational. Céline's prose disrupts the conventional subject-verb-object structure, the single rhythmic unit, and the clear distinction between speaker and addressee in order to incorporate unconscious drives in language.

Céline's writing reveals an author who clings to those social groups like women that both threaten and support his sense of identity. In this context, the figure of the Jew is as significant in his work as that of the mother. Although the Jew is not present in *Journey to the End of the Night*, he frequently appears in the other novels in which he plays a role that parallels the function of the Célinian mother. On one level, for Kristeva, Jews represent the social contract, as does the mother who gives birth to the next generation of citizens, because of their connection to the religion that is arguably the principal source of official Western culture. She demonstrates this in her psychoanalytic reading of Céline's novels. Yet the Jew functions primarily on another level for her as a deposed authority who becomes a victim in an anti-Semitic world, thus acquiring, like woman once again, the value of "impure body."

Her perspective on Céline, like her writing on China, has aroused considerable controversy, particularly by English critics who have accused her of anti-Semitism. Leslie Hill correctly understands anti-Semitism to be a threatening symptom Kristeva identifies in Céline's writing. For Hill, Kristeva reveals the limits of some forms of avant-garde political discourse emerging out of both a personal family drama and the Christian Holy Family.[4] In Kristeva's view, Céline's novels are neither misogynist nor anti-Semitic. On the contrary, she sees him staging dramas in which confrontations with women and Jews produce traumatic identity crises in a subject caught within the overly rigid hierarchies of Western societies dominated by a patriarch who is white and Christian. For this reason, the events and tone of *Powers of Horror* are primarily anxiety ridden and dangerous, producing a text that haunts the reader in ways that some of Kristeva's other writings, *About Chinese Women* and *The Samurai* for instance, do not.

The confrontation with the other that Kristeva finds in Céline is only in the end a joyous identification with woman, as the closing chapter of *Powers of Horror* reveals. This chapter also illuminates the concepts of nature and culture that structure her earlier and later writing and appear to create contradictions that have probably contributed to a misunderstanding of the political implications of her work. In *Revolution in Poetic Language*, for instance (see chapter 1 in this volume), Kristeva makes frequent reference to the role of culture, on the one hand, in the writer's choice of poetic devices enabling him primarily to identify with the mother and to subvert patriarchal authority. In addition, the movements toward both parents (and toward the androgynous figure that appears in the later *Black Sun*), present in the French Symbolists, suggest that cultural rather than biological factors are more significant. Lautréamont's musical scanning of sentences and complex logical operations derive primarily from the psychological, artistic, and philosophical practices of late nineteenth-century French life. In "Stabat Mater," on the other hand, one of the most discussed essays in *Tales of Love* (see chapter 1, p. 14; chapter 4, p. 65; and chapter 6, p. 109–11), the concept of nature is at the center of this prose poem on the universal bodily memory of close contact with the mother. The poem is printed parallel to a theoretical text on the ways in which the fantasy of motherhood shapes Western notions of femininity. For some critics who misunderstand her work, Kristeva valorizes nature over culture to such an extent that the writer is first and foremost a child who rejects nature in the form of the mother in order to identify with the father and thus comply with the social contract enabling him to write.[5] This criticism is more appropriately directed at Lacan's or Freud's theories in which there is a greater emphasis on the male as authority figure. For Kristeva, however, in the process of artistic creation, the writer–child struggles to recognize and identify with nature in the rejected power of woman.

A closer look at the nature/culture relation in *Powers of Horror* suggests subtle reasons to reject the view that nature plays the dominant role:

> If "something maternal" happens to bear upon the uncertainty that I call abjection, it illuminates the literary scription of the essential struggle that a writer (man or woman) has to engage in with what he calls demonic only to call attention to it as the inseparable obverse of his very being, the other (sex) that torments and possesses him. (208)

As this passage suggests, writing requires that you "identify against yourself" whether you are biologically male or female and whatever your sexual orientation. The process of creation is always masquerade—a struggle with the "demonic" that is the "obverse" of a conscious self. This "demon" is thus frequently, though not necessarily, the woman whom you confront and with whom you identify, the "something maternal" associated with abjection.

Although Kristeva does not use the words "nature" and "culture," she implies that nature plays a fundamental but limited role in the creative process. To the extent that each person possesses early symbiosis as bodily and psychic memory, every writer desires to replay that early moment of pleasure. Here she does not address the question of whether the writer's sex or sexual orientation in part determines the forms this replaying may take. She will do so later in *Feminine Genius*, in which, as Cynthia Chase has said of her earlier writing, Kristeva is committed "to analyzing the speaking subject—a sexual subject, yet one related only through the most complex mediations to gendered persons filling social roles."[6] At the same time she indicates in *Powers of Horror* and throughout her work the fundamental and dominant role of culture. Biology dictates neither the confrontation with woman nor how to manipulate the resources of a particular language in order to write. In the context of the radical differences that she stresses, Kristeva assumes a stance that is feminist and not essentialist, as the examination of the contradictory figure of the mother reveals in *Powers of Horror, About Chinese Women,* and *The Samurai.*

Kristeva went to China in 1974 with several other young intellectuals, members of the influential journal *Tel Quel*, eager to see and to examine firsthand the society transformed by Mao's Cultural Revolution. Upon her return, she wrote the book on Chinese women requested by the feminist publishing house L'Edition des femmes. *About Chinese Women* examines the history of women and the family in China beginning with an analysis of the author's Western orientation. Kristeva ends with a description of the women she met during her trip and with the suggestion she has offered throughout the book, that the West would do well to look to Chinese women as a model (195). Her first novel, *The Samurai*, replays the China adventure. The young writer, Olga, one of the protagonists, meets farmers, artists, and children during a trip to China in the early seventies. Kristeva describes her encounters with them, including their language and Taoist traditions.

China is literally and figuratively central in this novel of boundary-crossing. The section on the China trip follows the chapters on Olga's arrival in Paris from Eastern Europe and precedes the chapters on Olga's trip to New York. The People's Republic enables Kristeva to juxtapose capitalist and socialist societies while probing her past life. She comes to rethink, for example, her attitude toward children and childbearing. China also allows the novelist to represent, connect, and discuss historical events including Mao's Cultural Revolution and the French student and worker revolt of May '68 in which women played an important role. As in *About Chinese Women*, the East functions in this text as a historical marker pointing the way to both a more ethical and less repressed way of life for the West.

Much of Kristeva's theory and fiction, and especially *About Chinese Women* and *The Samurai*, bear the mark of 1974 and grow out of this historical and biographical moment. Thrown into turmoil and energized by the events of May '68, France was a place for intellectuals to write, often despite and against the state's authoritarianism under Pompidou and often informed by identity politics (women, gays, and prison inmates, for example, made important gains in the early seventies as documented in the newspaper *Libération*, first published in 1973). In this context, Kristeva's lyrical yet realistic representations of Chinese women, doing Tai Chi (98–99) or playing volleyball (195), for instance, enable the Western reader to imagine alternatives to everyday life that are more reflective, played out in a calmer rhythm, and linked to gender. Her reevaluation of Eastern and Western cultures and of women's role within them develops in *The Samurai* in which she describes Olga and Joelle's lives, for example, in their writing and relationship to their children.

Near the conclusion of *About Chinese Women*, Kristeva describes a women's volleyball game between China and Iran. The young Chinese women lose the game. They look like slim, young boys, are precise, and calm while, at the same time, appearing a little indifferent, as if playing in a dream. The Iranians win. They dominate the court with their size and show of passion. Each time they score a point they emit piercing screams and embrace feverishly. Kristeva uses the image of the volleyball game to describe Chinese and, visible in the Iranian women transformed by the Shah's White Revolution, European/American societies' influence in the Middle East. The fact that the Chinese women appear both female and male and that they are not wholly bent on winning the game is significant for the comparison and for the conclusion of the book. In this passage, the Chinese offer the possibility of a more competent, skillful, intelligent practice that succeeds better while seeming to fail.

Others do not read Kristeva in this way. Gayatri Spivak, to take a significant, well-known example, has attacked *About Chinese Women* on many fronts as inaccurate. In brief, she states that the notion of a matriarchal ancient China, an important component in Kristeva's presentation of Chinese history, is unlikely, that her discussion of Chinese literature is not sufficiently documented (137, 139), and that her reference to a monotheistic "West" does not take into account the case of India.[7]

Spivak also approaches Kristeva's work in a more general way as a kind of writing she calls "principled 'anti-feminism,'" describes *About Chinese Women* as supporting "the individualistic critical avant-garde," and suggests that the interest in China's past is nostalgic and apolitical (140). Spivak states that the effort to create a metaphysics of identity and to recuperate an origin (146) underlies Kristeva's book on China. Spivak is right to identify this component in Kristeva's work. It could be said, for example, that she values, above all else in her writing, reunion with the mother. As Spivak points out elsewhere in this discussion, Kristeva, like other postmodern cultural theorists, is engaged in a deconstruction of humanist discourse built on a rational male ego. In that context, it is not surprising that there is some nostalgia in her writing for a lost and different language. The search for origin, however, is only one of two basic impulses in her writing and alternates with the effort to exist in the symbolic discourse of realism and politics. Kristeva's analysis of China and the Jew help ground her writing in a symbolic discourse and a material history that is forward looking. While it is true that China's matriarchal history is not undisputed, that Kristeva's analysis of Chinese literature is sketchy, and that she does not consider a polytheistic India that has oppressed women for many years, Spivak's own analysis says little about matriarchy, history, and literature in this complex society. Nor does she undermine the book's primary contribution as an exploration of gender in China. Kristeva's comments in the prefatory note that she is "probing new regions of thought rather than providing answers," and that "prudence" "if not hesitation" "is warranted in any attempt to speak about women as well as about China,"[8] call attention to the difficulty of her subject and the care she takes in her treatment.

The opening of her book on China reflects Kristeva's French-Bulgarian frame of reference despite Spivak's claim to the contrary.[9] Kristeva gives a portrait of Western psychic formations and of women's predicament with some insight gained from her early years living in Bulgaria. With implicit acknowledgment of the influence of Marx and of the events of May '68, she sees women, like the working class, as a group marginalized by patriarchal institutions and a capitalist economy.

The more significant influence on this text and on all of her writing is clearly Sigmund Freud. From a neo-Freudian perspective, Kristeva describes how the biblical story of Eve's tempting of Adam shapes Western conceptions of women. Because of her role as seductress, Eve is punished, and is made to punish herself and to play a masochistic role because, while her nature leads her to satisfy desire, her need to exist in society entails that she accept the linguistic and narrative rules of the game to some extent. More specifically, she adopts an official social position appropriate to her secondary roles as wife and mother. At the same time, she must be wary of a stance that denies her nature as pleasure-seeking subject.

Following the summary of women's position in the West, Kristeva's examination of women and the family in China emphasizes their strength, an active role in sexuality and child care, and an association with the earth. According to her research and especially the work of Marcel Granet, China was probably a matrilineal and matrilocal peasant society before 1000 B.C.[10] Women used their own name after marriage and passed this name on to their children; matrimony took place with the cousin on the mother's side, and power resided with the women who did the farming in a mostly agricultural society. Reproduction for the community's survival along with the baby's need for its mother's attention for a relatively long time demanded that the woman play the major role in this culture. Burial customs, too, reflect dominance of women. The grandmother is often buried in the center of the burial ground with family members surrounding her. A larger quantity of fine pottery and jewelry accompanies her body compared to that of the man.

For Kristeva, the ancient Chinese worldview prior to 1000 B.C. did not subordinate or fuse woman to man as Chinese feudal beliefs, Confucianism, and Christianity later did. According to the concept of Li underpinning this culture, neither reason, associated with the masculine, nor matter, connected to the feminine, is above the other (reason and matter are in tension like the yin and yang of Taoism). In Chinese feudal society and Confucianism, as in the Judeo-Christian tradition, reason and a male authority figure dominate the physical world including the wife/mother.

From the tenth to the second century B.C., Chinese women endured the repressive atmosphere created by feudal morality and Confucius. While it seems at times that the history of repression is not unlike that faced later by Western women in countries having monotheistic, patriarchal psychic formations, Kristeva demonstrates that the subordination of women in China is probably different. The earlier matriarchal/matrilocal tradition, absent in France or the United States, for example, makes its presence felt in the struggle against feudal and Confucian thought. Taoism, dating from the sixth century B.C., the peasant revolts of the second century B.C., and the ancient rituals of Tai Chi are her principal examples of the resistance to the repression of women, a resistance drawing on a matriarchal past. Peasant revolts known as the "Yellow Turbans" and the "Red Eyebrows" fought for agrarian reforms in the name of Xi Wangmu, the Queen Mother of the West, and of Taoism, for instance.

Under Mao, Chinese women are able to recover more of their power in a society in the process of inventing a new form of social- ism. In 1974, Kristeva described desirable conditions in China that still are not commonly seen in the United States. In the interviews in the final section of the book, she discusses the likelihood that women combine intellectual and practical work, the availability of day care and paid maternity leave for all women, an education that teaches the child social skills, and art as part of everyday life. For Kristeva in 1974, these are conditions inaugurated by Mao and made possible in part by the legacy of matriarchy, disputed though it may be.

This legacy resurfaces in *The Samurai*, the title of which suggests the importance of the East, both Japan and China, in the novel. The principal protagonist is Olga, a young student arriving in Paris in the late sixties as the author did. Incorporating Kristeva's theory, Olga's psychoanalytic approach to work and to others (lover and later husband, Hervé, friend, Carole, and son, Alex, are the most significant others) enables her to live a satisfying life in Paris including a successful writing career and strong, reciprocal relationships.

Section three, "Chinese," recounts Olga's trip to China with Hervé, Bréhal, and other Parisian writers. She goes to China with few illusions. Like Kristeva herself, the product of a socialist country that at times denies freedom of expression to its writers, Olga is not the kind of Marxist Ivan assumes she is because she is from "down there." She is instead an Eastern European who, while influenced by Marx and critical of consumer society, appreciates Western civil rights and the impressive access to books in the Bibliothèque nationale. In the China of the mid-seventies, she discovers a country with more limited personal freedoms compared to the West (the writer's freedom of expression), but with the potential for creating a unique socialist society shaped by Taoist traditions. In this section, Olga, like Kristeva, reveals a subtlety of thought that avoids stereotypical responses both in her reflections on government and on the role of women in Chinese history. Intellectually honest, she cannot write the purely optimistic book on matriarchy in ancient China demanded by Bernadette for the Parisian feminist publishing house. This episode mirrors Kristeva's own break with some feminists in, for example, *Tales of Love* in 1983.

Olga ironically rediscovers her sense of self as a stranger under the gaze of women farmers in the town of Huxian. The women seem to consider Olga (and the other French writers who had come to study the "foreigners") as an extraterrestrial invading their planet. Olga is a foreigner both because she is in a country very different from her own along with friends who are from a second foreign country and because layers of her own psyche remain unknown to her.

She learns a lesson in painting during an encounter with a talented young cotton grower and her canvases. She becomes enamored of Chinese children to the extent that she realizes she not only does not dislike children as she had previously thought but also wants to become a mother. At the end of this section, she returns to Paris with the desire for a child and insights about language and Taoism to help Carole in the throes of a worsening depression.

Kristeva tells the story at times in the voice of the psychoanalyst, Joelle Cabarus, and at times in the voice of a third-person omniscient narrator. Through narrators informed by psychoanalysis and themselves fragments of the author's psyche, Kristeva identifies with and, to a lesser degree, distances herself from Olga and Joelle in an autobiographical novel and roman à clef of Parisian intellectuals of the sixties. The voices narrating Olga's life provide a framework for understanding her from Kristeva's multiple points of view.

Psychoanalytic theory underlies these points of view. The narrators frequently use indirect discourse and identify with the people they describe in an effort to understand both their conscious and unconscious selves. The dream of Bréhal (based on Roland Barthes, he is one of the colleagues visiting China with Olga and Hervé) while he sleeps on the bus during the China trip is an example of the omniscient narrator's voice identifying with the unconscious of another. After describing the dream in which Bréhal is arrested for trying to seduce a Chinese youth, the omniscient narrator discloses Olga's and Stanislas's comments on the nap. In what appears to be only amusing repartée, they analyze Bréhal's sleep in the context of their own quest for truth and pleasure. Poking fun at her own seriousness, Olga states that Bréhal's dreaming is a better way to explore the mind and China than their walking through the valley of the Statues and riding to Peking. Stanislas believes that Bréhal is "on the royal road to truth" and to death, withdrawing from the public world and indulging his instincts as a baby might indulge the appetites at the breast. While the tone of Olga's and Stanislas's remarks is joking, the narrator's multiple voices identify with Bréhal's unconventional dream while attempting to comprehend it.

By highlighting desire in a partly comic way, this episode reveals how psychoanalytic theory underpins the story and how China functions in it. Bréhal's funny attempt at seduction violates Chinese decorum and morality. The ensuing trial in the dream continues to do so as Bréhal borrows his defense from Sterdhal's Julien Sorel in *The Red and the Black*. Bréhal's dream enacts the repression of an individual freedom, the right to attempt a gay seduction—repression that the narrator's humorous treatment accepts as a fact of everyday life. While revealing this limitation on freedom, the episode ultimately conveys what Kristeva sees as most valuable in China—sexuality that is, to a greater extent than in the West, both male and female with neither sex dominating in the end. The young object of Bréhal's affection is "a fragile young man" who looked as if he were "made of porcelain" (164). When Bréhal reaches between the young man's knees, "the porcelain was frail and trembling: a known familiarity ["a familiar intimacy" would be closer to "une tendresse familière" (219 in the original)] was being refused. The lad was a victim of oppression, he certainly had need of love" (165). While contemporary Chinese culture is homophobic and represses sexuality to some degree, it also produces little machismo and an image of woman that is androgynous according to Kristeva. Bréhal and the young man are at Shanghai University watching dancers in a rehearsal of the Peking Opera: "manly girls with smooth calves, low-slung buttocks, and no breasts, whose arms swished through the air like swords. They never danced on their toes. Just a few bold leaps on feet that looked as versatile as hands" (164). The scene combines masculine and feminine elements. The women *and* men in the audience are porcelain dolls, the young man is trembling, and female dancers are manly, using their arms as swords and leaping boldly.

In this episode and throughout the novel, Olga grows as a writer, friend, and mother in her years of travel. Her behavior increasingly exemplifies the positive components in Kristeva's thinking and illustrates a political position implicit in it. This position appears in microcosm in *About Chinese Women* in which China is examined in ways that reveal its contradictions, complexities, and, in comparison to Western countries such as France and the United States, more egalitarian attitude toward gender, at least to hetero-sexuality. One of the women interviewed in the middle of the China chapter, Li Fenglan, is also a Party secretary who paints, alone and with a group of women. Her answers to Kristeva's questions on her painting focus on her status as woman along with the role of dreams:

> In fact, I don't paint the things I see, but I paint them from my dreams. . . . One must rise above what one sees. Besides, painting helps a woman to better herself. In the old times, women were held in contempt. The idea of a woman peasant-painter was absurd. Now we are happy, but I am happiest when I pick up my paintbrush. I tingle with excitement. (165)

While the Party contains many bureaucrats who serve to maintain the status quo, "grass-roots leaders" such as Li are intent on transformation and going beyond the psychic, economic, and familial limitations of patriarchal Chinese culture. The tone of the Li interview, like much of the rest of the book, is constructive and forward looking not nostalgic.

The unconscious, understood as a dangerous force in Kristeva's theory in *Powers of Horror* and later novels, never seriously affects the principal players in *About Chinese Women* or in *The Samurai*. Two exceptions from the former include the analysis of the "unimaginable suffering" and "moist eyes" of the elderly women with bound feet (81–85) and the housewives' workshop where the women are fearful and depressed (184).

In *The Samurai*, tragic possibilities are removed from the protagonists and played out in two minor characters, Martin and Carole. While Joelle suffers to some extent—especially from the unresponsiveness of her husband, Arnaud—like Olga, she is overall a strong woman who manages to achieve her professional and private goals. At the same time, Olga's successes are not utopian. As in Bréhal's dream, Kristeva connects the psychoanalytic theory underlying Olga's behavior to special circumstances in her character's (and in her own) life and to actual conditions in Paris, Eastern Europe, and China during the sixties. In Kristeva, psychoanalysis is both historical and material; as a theory and a practice, it does not distance Olga from the world but enables her to become engaged in the world via her writing and friendships.[11] *The Samurai* portrays Olga and Joelle as women living in a tumultuous era; their passions and ideas are shaped by a changing society, including family, friends school, the economy, the government, and especially the events of May '68 and the Chinese Cultural Revolution that helped bring about these events. Olga and Joelle are most often described as skillful and lucky players in a novel that becomes predictable despite the upheavals their environment helps create. Olga is, in the end, a character with whom many readers can empathize and whose projects arouse considerable reflection and admiration if not fear for her fate.

Most of Olga and Joelle's adventures in this novel, like the narrators' voices themselves, reveal an identification with another and the desire for a supportive feminine presence, a desire that finds satisfaction and success in writing. As Hervé puts it, "all belief begins with belief in the mystery of women, but some people don't give themselves up to it because they are able to express it" (37). While "don't give themselves up to it" appears ambiguous in that, in Kristeva's theory, one does precisely give up one's self in order to identify with the archaic mother, the clause becomes clear in the sense that such an identification is not ultimately masochistic because one finds a way to take control of one's life, that is, one is able to manipulate language, to communicate in and with the world.

While the most detailed identification and supportive presence in the novel is Olga's mothering of Alex, another example is more directly relevant to the role of China in Kristiva's work. At the end of her trip, Olga writes a note to Carole who is severely depressed. A supportive presence for her friend, she answers Carole's question "How do the Chinese say 'to believe'?":

"To believe" is *xinfu* in spoken Chinese; in written form: It is made up of "a man of his word" and "to marry" (or "to abandon oneself to"). No giving is involved, only a linking to the word. Begin rather by creating an empty space: *qixu* or   , and don't forget that emptiness isn't nothing—it's a tiger on a mound, the breath of the *yang* ready to leap on the "yin."

Look for that primive emptiness inside yourself; we'll try to find it together. (209)

Olga's advice to Carole resonates in the context of not only the Chinese episodes focusing on matriarchy and childbearing but also much of the novel and Kristeva's writing in the three works examined in this chapter. Hervé's obituary for his father, for example, used Master Eckert's words, "As long as a man has space within him, he also has *difference*" (295). Both Olga and Hervé borrow an image with female connotations from Taoism and Eckert. Olga draws on what she has come to see as a Chinese view of sexuality that includes an intermingling of feminine and masculine without fusion: the "feminine" inner space becomes the yang ready to spring on the yin.

On a level darker and more problem ridden than that of *About Chinese Women* and *The Samurai*, Kristeva's project from *Revolution in Poetic Language* in 1974 to at least *Black Sun* in 1987, and clearly in *Powers of Horror* and in the later novels *The Old Man and the Wolves* (1991) and *Possessions* (1996), and in her recent trilogy, as I will show in chapter 7, has been to lay out a similar political position.[12] In her theory she develops Freudian concepts and shows how literary texts stage psychic dramas in which identifications with male and female figures are prominent.

Jacqueline Rose examines the dark tone of much of Kristeva's theory up to 1983 in one of the best essays on her earlier work. Referring to *Tales of Love*, for example, she says that one should not dismiss Kristeva's analysis of love. Instead, love in her theory can be linked to a political practice not unlike that of *About Chinese Women*. Rose sees Kristeva's writing

as a strategy which allows individual subjects to negoti-
ate the troubled psychic waters which she herself so
graphically describes. To which we could add that this
love does not have to be incompatible with politics. Did
not Kristeva herself say that without love of women
there was no point in going to China in 1974?[13]

Thus, as Rose suggests, China (and I would add, the figure of
the Jew) plays a substantial role in Kristeva's work, illuminating her
version of a psychoanalytic writing as a feminist identity politics.
The persistence of the image of a matriarchal society, the interac-
tion of yang/yin in Taoism, Mao's Cultural Revolution, and the figure of the Jew provide a historical framework for the exploration of
psychic formations in East and West both in her cultural theory
and fiction in *About Chinese Women, Powers of Horror,* and *The Samurai.* The components of Kristeva's thinking that I have examined
here, including the focus on subjectivity and writing rather than on
institutions and on social activisim, the notion of the woman as
nurturing "origin" and often as abject foreigner, may appear ahistorical, apolitical, or even masochistic. Yet her writing in these three
texts and as a whole is grounded in actual events, keenly aware of
the distribution of power, and bent on radical change.

❦ 6 ❧

Kristeva's Work in the Eighties: A New Space for Woman and Love

Tales of Love (*Histoires d'amour*, 1983), *In the Beginning Was Love: Psychoanalysis and Faith* (*Au Commencement était l'amour: Psychanalyse et foi*, 1985), and *Black Sun: Depression and Melancholia* (*Soleil noir: Dépression et mélancholie*, 1987) are texts of remarkable intensity in which the reader senses danger between the lines.[1] Kristeva's writing in the eighties describes a mother who provides for her children while at times portraying her as an abject figure linked to melancholy, masochism, and the death drive as in *Powers of Horror* (see chapter 5 in this volume). The father now reenters her work primarily as a life-affirming figure rather than as a censor.

These texts return periodically to the image of the parents wielding power over the child. Critics continue to charge that Kristeva's approach, like all psychoanalysis, reduces choice, as well as historical and cultural difference, to biological necessities. For such critics, she ties behavior to early relationships to the parents and particularly to the father as the pivotal authority figure.[2] There is, in fact, an increasing presence of the maternal figure in this phase of her writing. More often than not, Kristeva stresses the intervention of female figures, for example, in the case histories that are also primarily of female patients. Similarly, her recent trilogy emphasizes the influence of the mother and focuses on three female thinkers, Hannah Arendt, Melanie Klein, and Colette.

In the eighties, Kristeva's psychoanalytic approach returns to its Freudian roots in the therapy and mental care of individuals. Substantial sections of these three works, and especially *Black Sun*, analyze her patients' and her own personal experience. The addition of this experience in the volumes treated here, particularly the case histories of her female patients, contributes to the solidity of her theory and to an already impressive diversity in the fields she studies. In words conveying her own view of Freud's influence on her work, one could say that psychoanalysis functions as a flexible material base for her theory because the early symbiotic relation to the mother is fundamental as is the therapeutic practice that acknowledges the role of this relation. Kristeva demonstrates more forcefully than ever that a psychoanalytic model recognizing the importance of early physical experience enables her, as it does Freud, to do genuinely interdisciplinary work in art, religion, and everyday life.

Kristeva's politics grows out of a theory of subjectivity describing but not limiting itself to the dynamics of the individual psyche. Her work is part of the critical debate that, since the sixties, has turned from American New Criticism and French Structuralism. While providing insight into structural patterns, these formalisms often denied the role of the political, historical, and psychological in literature, and thus reduced the dynamic human spirit incorporated in the text. Kristeva's understanding of subjectivity is formalist in that she pays attention to textual structures apparently separate from content, Structuralist in that she links these formations to more general social patterns, Freudian and Bakhtinian in that she discovers psychic conflict, dialogism, and political affiliations at the core of the text.

Beyond Western ideology's apparent belief in the individual's freedom, literary theorists and critics, including Kristeva, increasingly see their work as part of an interdisciplinary project with a political dimension: supporting the right of individuals and groups to self-determination and affirming cultural and gender difference. Developments in the fields of Women, Gender, and Cultural Studies emphasizing emergent literatures and women, gay, and minority authors are examples of this belief and of the institutional changes that writing may help bring about. A consideration of the political implications of these books thus sheds light on Kristeva's project in connection with a certain tendency in the academy, at least in the United States and Europe, since the sixties.

Within a loose chronology that advances from Plato, *The Song of Songs,* and Ovid through Bernard De Clairvaux, Mozart, and Shakespeare to Baudelaire, Stendhal, Freud, and Bataille, to name just a few, *Tales of Love* also moves backward in time from Mallarmé to the Bible, for example, mirroring the dynamics of a shifting psyche. The opening statement itself incorporates theory within that dynamics as Kristeva describes her book on love as a defense mechanism to protect her own personal experience.

After a first reading during which one might wonder why she has selected these particular texts, Kristeva's range of reference coupled with the depth of her insights persuasively demonstrates the validity and usefulness of her theory in understanding the phenomenon of love in Western cultures. While her analysis includes many texts that seem to be unrelated to each other, it is precisely Kristeva's theoretical flair that enables her to make the connections among them as I show in the following analysis.

She finds the seeds of a contemporary psychological crisis in Plato: the inability to recreate an identification with the imaginary loving father. *The Symposium* and *Phaedrus* present love as idealization, a linking of physical desire to a recognition of the spiritual and good. Later on, in Ovid's version of the myth of Narcissus in *Metamorphoses,* and especially in Plotinus's use of the myth in the *Enneads,* Plato's process of idealization becomes internalized. In loving, you seek the good in yourself, in an image that you objectify. Desire for the self continues to drive the psyche once you find that you cannot possess this object.

In an examination that is both local and more global, both personal and general, she analyzes the evolution of Western love while returning periodically to that of the subject moving toward the acquisition of language. Her study of Plato and Ovid demonstrates how the psyche comes to desire an impossible love in its quest for both physical satisfaction and moral approval in an other that is also the self. The subject in this way identifies not with a loving imaginary father, but rather one who condemns physical love as he or she progresses to the Oedipal stage, the critical moment in the neo-Freudian model underlying Kristeva's theory.

Synthesizing complex bodies of thought, she describes how classical, Judaic, and Christian ideas come together in shaping love and subjectivity. Her creative reading of *The Song of Songs* reveals how this enigmatic biblical poetry prefigures the internalizing of Narcissistic love and reinforces its masculine character. Kristeva convincingly links Narcissus who seeks his object in himself and in the good to the bride who seeks her object in submission to a fleeing male authority figure, though one might object that she neglects sexual difference in linking the (male) Narcissus and the (female) bride in this way. Both Judaic and classical love leave the subject longing for an object that can be possessed only through separation from the body. In *The Song of Songs*, God is ultimately the fleeing figure one can never hold; in Ovid's and Plotinus's Narcissus myth, the unattainable object is a beautiful image of oneself. For Kristeva, these three texts are impossible scenarios, unfolding the process of internalization that the subject undergoes in acquiring language as a substitute for the mother. In the end, they cumulatively reveal the subject withdrawing into himself or herself in an attempt to find a transcendent being.

Kristeva traces this withdrawal up to Bataille and, within the outline of an overall category of love that grows increasingly dominant in Western cultures, succeeds in recognizing the specificity of individual texts while identifying those who contradict that category at the very moment when they seem to voice the notion of a body-less self. Her treatment of Bernard De Clairvaux's sermons is a good example.

Twelfth-century mysticism, and especially Bernard's sermons, are to some degree free of the rational male authority figure that the Bible locates in Christ. Bernard stresses the inevitable eruption of emotions and especially of animal sensations along the shaky path to salvation; for Kristeva, his work violates the concept of love as a separation from the body.

Distancing herself from the Freud who was not receptive to Dora's insight at the end of the famous case history, Kristeva reveals her sense of language as a system open to the discoveries of both analyst and analysand. The overall orientation toward the psyche's stages (Oedipal and so on) as he or she acquires language, along with Kristeva's theories of love and of the imaginary father continue to be shaped by both Freud and Lacan. Before and after describing the relative freedom of those writers who undercut the dominant fantasy of love as a denial of the body, Bernard and Jeanne Guyon, for instance, Kristeva follows Freud in her theory of the subject in the first part of *Tales of Love* as she indicates: "The receptive mind of a disappointed Goethian Jew, living in Central Europe between the two wars, continues to be the only one to come forward as capable of fitting out—with considerable risk and uncertainty—a new space for love" (61). While Freud's and Lacan's theories are overall most valuable for the considerable extent to which they recognize and are able to listen to the other, unlike Freud at the end of "Dora," and unlike Lacan in his coming to believe that the unconscious can be contained by language, especially by mathematics, Kristeva takes on "risk and uncertainty" in this book as she discusses psychoanalysis' role in shaping contemporary notions of love. She does not give priority to psychoanalysis as a discourse that yields truth with the psychoanalyst "in the position of knowledge" as Leslie Hill states, unless one acknowledges that the language of analysis goes in search of its own meaning.[3] Like the speech of analyst and analysand that are open to each other, her analysis of love and the case studies of her patients constitute open systems in which each both receives and gives insights. Her defense of subjectivity goes further than Freud's and Lacan's, at least in some of their texts, in that she acknowledges the emergence of the subject into the "object" of analysis. The analyst Kristeva becomes the analysand.

In what may be her strongest theoretical writing to 1977 when it first appeared, she describes the emergence of the subject into an apparently objective analysis in the chapter "Stabat Mater." She devotes the chapter to the experience of motherhood both in itself and as the source of one of psychoanalysis' major assumptions: there is a material base underlying the mother's role and anchoring Western dramas of love, the bodily experience connecting her to the child. Much of the chapter's content and form follow on and expand the analysis of love begun earlier in the book. Briefly stated, "Stabat Mater" studies (1) the mother as fantasy linking her to the body, nonlanguage, and the unnamable; and (2) Western patriarchy and its struggle to reject the maternal, for example, in the evolution of the Christian notion of an impossible love, with its source in *The Song of Songs,* into the relationship with a virgin, with its peak in medieval Europe; a musical example, Pergolesi's version of the Latin hymn incorporating the dying son's love for the Virgin Mary gives this essay its title, "Stabat Mater" (Stood the Mother).

What is most thought-provoking in the chapter is the break with the predominantly abstract, impersonal analysis outlined above, a break prefigured by Kristeva, the psychoanalyst, interrupting her theory primarily to present her patients' case histories. In "Stabat Mater" she juxtaposes to the analysis a kind of prose poem that speaks personally and concretely about the experience of motherhood before it merges with the abstract description of the mother's dual existence in matter and language:

> Yet the eye picked up nothing, the ear remained deaf. But everything swarmed, and crumbled, and twisted, and broke—the grinding continued. . . . Then, slowly, a shadowy shape gathered, became detached, darkened, stood out: seen from what must be the true place of my head, it was the right side of my pelvis. Just bony, sleek, yellow, misshapen, a piece of my body jutting out unnaturally, asymmetrically, but slit: severed scaly surface, revealing under this disproportionate pointed limb the fibers of a marrow. . . . Frozen placenta, live limb of a skeleton, monstrous graft of life on myself, a living dead. Life. . . . death . . . undecidable. During delivery it went to the left with the afterbirth . . . My removed marrow, which

nevertheless acts as a graft, which wounds but increases me. Paradox: deprivation and benefit of childbirth. But calm finally hovers over pain, over the terror of this dried branch that comes back to life, cut off, wounded, deprived of its sparkling bark. The calm of another life, the life of that other who wends his way while I remain henceforth like a framework. Still life. There is him, however, his own flesh, which was mine yesterday. Death, then, how could I yield to it? (242–43)

Breaking Western societies' relative silence on the subject of childbirth, Kristeva creates a prose poem describing a visceral experience filled with contradiction: the baby is a "severed scaly surface" that is at once both part of her ("a piece of my body jutting out") and separate from her ("live limb of a skeleton"), both alive and dead. More precisely, in the context of this discussion, the passage quoted above is a good example of Kristeva's attempt in "Stabat Mater" to recreate within her book on love an identification with an imaginary loving father. The passage combines elements of the replaying of the pleasurable symbiosis with the mother (a slit body, a feeling of calm) with those of the functioning of the symbolic (a pointed limb, a male baby). Finally, after the discussion of the mother's material and linguistic experience, the prose poem reemerges, first from the child's point of view and then from the woman's, to affirm a heterogeneous life in the body and in speech that can be discovered in the mother and, more generally, in ourselves. If Kristeva speaks so often of the imaginary or loving father in *Tales of Love*, and later in *In the Beginning Was Love* and *Black Sun*, it is because the male has been made over through contact with the female, becoming a mixture of genders. In the following passage, the woman makes clear that existence is not monolithic, it is a complex web of bodily and symbolic language:

Women doubtless reproduce among themselves the strange gamut of forgotten body relationships with their mothers. Complicity in the unspoken, connivance of the inexpressible, of a wink, a tone of voice, a gesture, a tinge, a scent. We are in it, set free of our identification papers and names, on an ocean of preciseness, a computerization of the unnamable. No communication between individuals but connections between atoms, molecules, wisps of words, droplets of sentences. (257)

Kristeva uses the prose poem, part of which appears above, to enact a break with the dominating discourse of love that, to the extent that it is abstract and of one piece, threatens to deny the role of the body to her very own words, much as the tyrannical father functions in the Oedipal complex.

The conclusion of *Tales of Love* expresses the risk but also the potential benefit that accompanies such a break. Once again signaling a difference with Lacan if not with Freud (379), Kristeva speaks of psychoanalysis "as the instrument of a departure from . . . enclosure, not as its warden." She fears the risk of finding herself "in unstable, open, undecidable spaces" but decides to run that risk in the hope of alleviating pain and of "trigger[ing] a discourse" where "emptiness" and "out-of placeness become essential elements . . . of a *work in progress*."

In an apparently simpler form, *In the Beginning Was Love: Psychoanalysis and Faith* explores the risky business of writing "a *work in progress*." This book confines itself to religion and psychoanalysis, lays out assumptions and definitions omitted in Kristeva's other books, and is brief (sixty-three pages). For those who have read *Tales of Love*, some of *In the Beginning Was Love* retraces familiar ground—for instance, the analysis of the destructive fantasy of the Virgin Mother in the Catholic cult of Mary and in the case histories of contemporary French women who live in a culture that talks very little about motherhood and, through its silence, allows that fantasy to continue.

In the Beginning Was Love ventures into new territory, though, as it explores the process of psychoanalysis as a therapeutic method that can help others and oneself to live more creatively and more happily by moving closer to an identification with a loving rather than a domineering father. Describing her initial reaction to the invitation to lecture on the topic "Psychoanalysis and Faith" to the students at Sainte-Geneviève, a Catholic high school in Versailles, as a "recoiling," Kristeva explains that the topic denies psychoanalysis' autonomy by subordinating it to another discipline. Instead of declining the invitation because of the unacceptable topic, she decides to study the rhetoric that lies behind it, that is, to analyze the oppositional relationship between psychoanalysis and Catholicism. In doing so, she demonstrates that psychoanalysis, like Catholicism, does not have priority as a discourse that yields truth. Rather, it is a system that is open to "the truth" of other discourses, in this case, to that of her Catholic audience. In other words, she shows that, in the end, subject and object are shifting entities.

Strict adherence to the tyrannical father in her writing would mean remaining enclosed within a homogeneous analytic language, steering clear of the suffering of her patients and herself alike, and in this volume, of the Catholic rhetoric that subordinates psychoanalysis to religious belief either directly or as an oppositional discourse, as a rejection of such belief. To include case histories as well as her personal experience and to read the rhetoric of psychoanalysis in the light of Catholicism and vice versa is to try to lift repression and to create a space for a loving father.

The opening sections of *In the Beginning Was Love* talk about cringing at the lecture topic, rejecting Catholicism as a young girl, and her patient Paul. More convincingly than the content, the form of the work risks sacrificing the autonomy of the analytic method by placing religion on a par with psychoanalysis and attempting to learn more about her approach by studying Catholicism. After taking on the apparently inappropriate topic, she explains how belief can sometimes recreate an identification with a loving father, a recreation that psychoanalysis is only now trying to achieve—her own work is an example.

In the context of the volume and her work as a whole, the identification achieved within a Christian framework is limited: only some people today and primarily mystic writers in the twelfth century believe in God in a manner that retains the strong sensual component that enables an identification with the imaginary father. Her own rejection is far more typical of the contemporary intellectual's reaction to faith. Bringing together the concepts of a Christian God and sensuality is an arduous task as Jeffrey Kripal also makes clear in discussing the ways in which the predominantly masculine associations with God in Catholicism can make a contemporary mystical relation difficult for a heterosexual male.[4] In her lectures to the students at Sainte-Geneviève, Kristeva opens her writing to alternative possibilities for religion when offered an occasion for dialogue with a Christian audience.

In the section, "Credence-credit," for instance, Kristeva's analysis of Catholicism interrupts itself to reveal her own fantasies as a teenager trying to experience faith. In this way, psychoanalysis turns back on itself as object of its analysis and becomes subordinate to the autobiography that, in the end, shows how religion may be seen as a fantasy that, on some occasions, has satisfied the psychic needs of contemporary people to unite with a loving father.

In the Beginning Was Love, then, is a book that produces knowledge about her audience and herself: at least some in her Catholic audience are apparently able to lift the repression and guilt that she and many others have experienced in their attempts to practice a religion. The volume also produces an insight into psychoanalysis: it is most creative when it folds back on itself and lies open to other systems. Kristeva herself indicates that she is not engaged in a so-called scientific inquiry claiming to maintain a "neutral" point of view, as does the positivist, but rather an inquiry claiming that point of view plays a role in constituting the very "object" under study.

If Kristeva's reinvention of psychoanalysis in *Tales of Love* and *In the Beginning Was Love* implies that the beginning of political activity consists in achieving a tentative independence within oneself, then *Black Sun* takes a closer look at what may be the most difficult moment, especially for the female, who must identify with a figure whose sex is not her own, in the process of achieving that independence. This volume focuses on a stage in psychic evolution when one stops at the threshold of loving the imaginary father. Development comes to a halt as melancholy sets in, causing the subject to deny separation from the mother and to suffer from a catastrophic linguistic problem—language that conveys neither emotion nor ideas.

Like Freud whose analysis of patients enables him to develop a more general model of psychic development, Kristeva's study of Anne, Marie-Ange, and Isabel helps her construct a model for both them and others as she examines the trauma of learning language and the depressive states experienced when language becomes difficult. In this context, the melancholic woman, like Anne, for example, who constantly mourns the "lost object" that is her mother, becomes a metaphor for human beings as they fail to forge an effective language during temporary bouts of severe depression.

As in the two preceding books, Kristeva combines a psychoanalysis of disciplines (painting, literature, and religion) with that of her patients and succeeds in showing the suffering and temporary fulfillment that give shape to the subject speaking in both domains. In the course of this double discourse, she reveals the pretensions of the painters and writers, while lending dignity to the patients (*Tales of Love*, 17). Here she includes primarily new readings of Hans Holbein, Gérard De Nerval, Fyodor Dostoevsky, and Marguerite Duras, along with case histories of Anne, Marie-Ange, and Isabel.

While it is clear that the artists create work impossible for the patients to produce, it is equally clear that the artists' texts yield fuller insight into human pain and pleasure when studied alongside the patients' texts or case histories. She describes the juxtaposition of theory and case history as an attempt "to open up the amorous experience of the speaking being to the complex gamut of his untenable passion, paradise and hell included. Neither denying the ideal, nor forgetting its cost." The sixteenth-century German painter Holbein is one of her most vivid examples of the way she uses art to more fully explore the psyche. For Kristeva, Holbein is a melancholic who achieves a provisional sense of fulfillment in his painting *The Dead Christ*. One of the artists located at critical transitions in the development of Western thought whom Kristeva has identified (Antoine DeLaSale and Mikhail Bakhtin are examples from her earlier work), Holbein leaves behind more orthodox Christian art, identifies with a dead mother, and recreates her in his grim version of Christ on the cross. Underlying Holbein's achievement is a struggle to represent what is nonrepresentable in the Christian era in which he lives—death with no hope of eventual transcendence. One recalls the memento mori included in his *Ambassadors*, one of the paintings made more familiar by John Berger's well-known study of the image in the West, *Ways of Seeing*.

Holbein's struggle, especially as represented in his painting *The Dead Christ* becomes more tangible and vivid when considered as a version of that of Anne, Kristeva's patient. Examining his canvases, his life, and the Reformation, she explains how Holbein's attempts to reveal an unnamable melancholy constitute an identification with a dead mother. Kristeva juxtaposes her account of *The Dead Christ* to the analysis of Anne at the end of a sequence of theoretical writing and case studies, a position enabling the reader to perceive the personal, immediate quality of both Anne's and Holbein's melancholia.

A successful anthropologist, Anne experiences long bouts of depression when she withdraws to her bed for days, unable to speak or eat. During analysis, Anne talks primarily about these bouts, her childhood skin diseases that demanded that she not have contact with her mother, and a dream of a Klaus Barbie–type trial in which Barbie is found guilty, to Anne's relief. Kristeva discovers that behind Anne's struggle to reveal what is nonrepresentable, the denial of separation from her mother, and behind the lack of emotion and partial incoherence in Anne's words, is melancholy and anger towards the mother, expressed not in the content but rather in the etymology and tone of voice of those words. Once Anne sees this, she is able to connect her low self-esteem to that early denial, to talk about the source of her withdrawals, and to analyze a dream in which she gives birth to a little girl with her mother's face who represents the fragile new life she is ready to begin after analysis.

What Holbein has in common with Anne is the recreation of a stage of melancholy and powerlessness in psychic development when he refuses to separate from a dead mother. In his case, the birth of a son who represents the new generation of painters to replace him and the friendship with Erasmus that influenced his loss of orthodox faith probably arouse a fear of death and help explain this stage. The rise of the Reformation and especially of Martin Luther, whose iconoclasm made the image of a loving, life-giving Christ impossible, further explains his feelings of powerlessness. In this context, Holbein denies the separation from the mother that would enable him to move forward to identification with a loving father much as Anne denies separation from, clings to and attacks the mother who abandoned her as a child. Ultimately, each does progress to this vital identification: Holbein in achieving his minimalist painting, Anne in the conclusion of her analytic "cure."

Kristeva writes:

> Could it be superego voluntarism that maintains the image of an oblatory Father, or is it the commemoration of an archaic paternal figure arisen from the paradise of primary identifications? The forgiveness inherent in Redemption condenses death and resurrection and presents itself as one of the most interesting and innovative instances of trinitary logic. The key to the nexus seems to be primary identification: the oral and already symbolic oblatory gift exchanged between Father and Son. . . .
>
> Did Holbein become the painter of such a Christian thought, stripped of its antidepressive carrier wave, and amounting to identification with a regarding beyond? He leads us, at any rate, to the ultimate edge of belief, to the threshold of nonmeaning. The *form* (of art) alone gives back serenity to the waning of forgiveness, while love and salvation take refuge in the execution of the work. Redemption would simply be the discipline of a rigorous technique. (135)

In her description of "the commemoration of an archaic paternal figure arisen from the paradise of primary identification" and "the threshold of nonmeaning" where "artistic form" suggests "serenity," "love," and "salvation," it becomes clear that Holbein's painting dramatizes an identification with a loving father who combines the positive characteristics of mother and father for the child/subject. This dramatization in paint constitutes a "resurrection" for Holbein in the way that *El Desdichado* does for Nerval. The Christian desire for an afterlife becomes the artist's desire for a language (words or paint) that confronts "the Black Sun of Melancholia" (169).

Kristeva's theory of subjectivity in these three books aims to have her patients and readers along with herself achieve a greater share of autonomy. Her psychoanalytic method and model, emphasizing the need to identify with the loving father, moves the subject away from enclosure within a language that is primarily rational and unitary toward a more flexible speech that is courageous enough to be at times irrational and divided. She allows the subject to emerge in the object of her analysis (*Tales of Love*), subordinates psychoanalysis to religion (*In the Beginning Was Love*), and shows how it is possible for both a painter and a mentally ill woman to confront a psychological drama they must at the same time hide in order to exist (*Black Sun*).

In an article that recognizes the complexity of Kristeva's theory and does not impose a new conservatism on her work, including *Tales of Love*, Jacqueline Rose surveys the development of her writing as a whole. She applauds Kristeva's work for including sexuality, politics, and the unconscious in an analysis of people and texts.[5] While agreeing with Kristeva's rejection of political theory that sees social structures as monolithic, she does not agree that feminism is necessarily such a theory. She finds fault with Kristeva's dismissal of feminism and with her positing the mother and more generally the semiotic as something female that Western cultures repudiate in order to exist. Fearful that such an assumption reinforces the gender stereotypes that have denied autonomy to women, Rose rejects those parts of Kristeva's theory that have the mother function in this way. I would point out that in Kristeva's work in the eighties the repudiation of the abject mother is only the first part of a movement including not only repudiation (as Rose indicates) but also reunion. The identification with a loving father that she describes in Holbein's *The Dead Christ* is ultimately a recreation, within a sign, of the early symbiosis with the mother. In this framework, the repudiation of the abject mother in *Black Sun* is part of a dual movement that goes on indefinitely as the psyche constructs and deconstructs its fragile identity.

With reservations about her elaboration of the semiotic, especially because of its potential for reinforcing gender stereotypes, Rose nevertheless suggests that Kristeva's version of psychoanalysis is worthy of attention precisely because it raises questions about the persistence of such stereotypes in fantasy, including Kristeva's own. Rose stresses the importance of contradictory psychic structures as distinct from but not unrelated to social structures equally rife with conflict in Kristeva. She concludes, "Her [Kristeva's] work gives us the measure of the difficulties when politics tries to open itself up to the ravages of the unconscious mind" (164).

Kristeva's writing in the eighties raises questions about both the persistence of stereotypes and the linking of the unconscious to those who are socially marginal. She demonstrates that, by turning inward to become more aware of what one has repressed, and by creating oneself, including the unconscious, in language, the individual makes others more conscious as well. Such creation is a form of existing in the world and of functioning politically so that individuals may exercise a degree of control over the flow of desire. Kristeva writes in the concluding chapter of *Tales of Love*, "While waiting for social institutions to integrate such extraterrestrials, those survivors of primary narcissism, it is still in the imagination and symbolic realizations that their faltering identity will best find a way to construct itself as necessarily false—imaginary" (380). In the spirit of *Tales of Love, In the Beginning Was Love,* and *Black Sun* considered as a whole, these words affirm a significant degree of self-determination for the individual and for institutions.

7

Fiction, Fact, and Theory: The World as Flesh and Blood

Julia Kristeva's fiction—*The Samurai* (1990), *The Old Man and the Wolves* (1991), and *Possessions* (1996) and her recent trilogy, *Feminine Genius: Life, Madness, Words—Hannah Arendt, Melanie Klein, and Colette* (1999-2002)—are explorations of female psyches grappling with writing, sexual passion, motherhood, death, and history. Together, these works compel a reading of Kristeva's work as a feminist politics offering possibilities for reshaping personal and public life in Western societies at the beginning of the twenty-first-century.[1] Revealing sexist practices, Kristeva focuses on the category "woman," at times in the body of a man, and thus does so without essentializing. This final chapter on her recent work examines more fully the corpus of Kristeva's contributions to psychoanalytic writing and the ways in which her version of a feminist politics subverts the gendered hierarchies of contemporary life.

On a level darker and more problem ridden than that of *The Samurai* and *About Chinese Women*, Kristeva's writing from *Revolution in Poetic Language* in 1974 to *Black Sun* in 1987, and, more recently in her novels and trilogy on women writers, delineates psychic formations and develops a political position (see chapter 5, p. 1). *Revolution*, for example, demonstrates how Mallarmé reenacts

121

personal dilemmas in scenarios that are at once familial and part of the social and cultural history of the working classes under the upper-middle-class state led by Louis Napoleon (see chapter 1). In this chapter dealing with her recent work, she revises Freudian concepts, especially that of the father of individual pre-history, and reveals how writing, and in particular autobiographical fiction, stages psychic dramas in which identifications with primarily female figures are prominent.

Kristeva hones her storytelling skills in her last two novels in which the unconscious unleashes pain and aggression to a much greater extent than in *The Samurai*. In *The Old Man and the Wolves*, Kristeva describes a city in Eastern Europe—Santa Varvara—that has been invaded by wolves, a reference, it would seem, to the Soviet armies and to the Gothic tradition of werewolves in Eastern European and Russian literature. Many of the citizens, who spend a good deal of their time watching television or fighting with each other, come to resemble the animals in this science fiction/philosophical tale, or, as Kristeva herself describes her fiction, "polar metaphysique" (metaphysical murder mystery).[2]

Through the eyes of Parisian journalist Stephanie Delacour, Kristeva examines the writing process and a psychology that seems similar to her own. In *The Old Man*, as the title suggests, she focuses mostly on an atypical Santavarvaran, a Latin professor, Septicius Clarus, who was the first to be aware of and to fight the wolves. Having returned to cover political events in Santa Varvara where she lived for a time when her father was ambassador, Delacour is now committed to telling the story of the wolves' invasion.

Like Septicius, Delacour understands the threat of the wolves and of the increasingly aggressive people, especially the cruel doctor, Vespasian. Her friend Alba, Vespasian's lover, who had originally been the only other person to take Septicius's fight against the animals seriously, soon begins to undergo the metamorphosis. The professor is distraught to learn that he, too, is becoming a wolf. Throughout the novel, the principal characters—Stephanie, Septicius, and Alba—possess and, to different degrees, grapple with the wolves, a force threatening them from within and without. In the psychoanalytic context of Kristeva's work, the image of the wolf gives shape to violence arising from both tyrannical political leaders and from the death drive within.

During her visit to Santa Varvara, Delacour renews her friendship with Alba and particularly with Septicius. When he dies after becoming sick and hospitalized, she attempts to find out if Vespasian or Alba has murdered him as she suspects. In the end, despite some uncertainties, she reaffirms her commitment to tell the story of the crimes of the wolves.

Kristeva weaves a tale that appears to be intensely personal, and at the same time, broadly political. Like the author herself in 1991 when Stoyan Kristeva dies, her spokeswoman, Delacour, both mourns and celebrates the life of her loving father as she tells the story of the Old Man. Septicius is an androgynous figure who seems to resemble Kristeva's own father and also Freud's father of individual pre-history.[3] A nurturing presence, he joins Delacour in gardening, "feed[ing her]." On the same page, she describes her father in terms that are equally maternal: "he loved like a flower open to the blessing of dawn-warmed dew" (168). In the frame of both the novel and of this chapter on Kristeva's recent fiction and trilogy, Septicius represents "the feminine" or good mother who provides early emotional support for Delacour. Thus, it is not the feminine in a biological sense but rather associations made with the concept of the mother as throughout much of Kristeva's writing, for example, in "Motherhood According to Giovanni Bellini" (*Desire in Language*). The Old Man also opposes the wolves, icon par excellence of "the masculine," associated not only with an animal preying on women, but also, in this novel, with an oppressive figure of authority, frequently a life-threatening form of communism or capitalism.

The Old Man stages a familial drama, especially the loss of a beloved father, in its social contexts. The protagonist, Delacour, situates the events after the fall of the Berlin Wall, as capitalism à l'Américaine quickly crosses all boundaries. It soon becomes clear that the wolves are not primarily the Soviet armies, but rather a version of capitalism and, ultimately, of the death drive that is even more dangerous.

Like *The Samurai, The Old Man and the Wolves* is a novel that stands on its own and can be more fully understood in its connections to Kristeva's life and theory. Part 1, "The Invasion" reveals the Old Man suffering in a Santa Varvara under siege. Through her soon-to-be-revealed narrator, Delacour, Kristeva identifies with Septicius attacked by the wolves. Delacour relives the suffering and pleasurable moments of the Old Man even as he lives through his former student.

While it is the masculine and the death drive represented in the wolves that is perhaps most palpable in this novel, the feminine and sensual pleasure represented in Septicius play a vital role. Kristeva uses the voice of Billie Holiday, who obsesses Septicius nearly as much as the wolves do, to create a feminine presence in the Old Man. In an early passage depicting Septicius, her voice is described as "flesh-and-blood," "milk-chocolate," singing appropriately enough, "My mother, she gave me something" (24). Later, at the moment of Septicius's death, still surrounded by the wolves, he is "overwhelmed" by Holiday's voice, filled with a joy described as both childish and sexual. The last few words of this chapter recount Septicius's death through the ear, a womblike organ associated with conception and death, as Delacour explains (123). Septicius's character will overlap with that of Delacour's father in the third section on his death.

In part 2, "Detective," Delacour reveals her identity and investigates the city and the killing that both she and Septicius had dreaded. Having arrived in Santa Varvara to cover human rights violations and the invasion of the wolves, she discovers the murder of a girl on the beach who resembles Alba. She also comes to believe that Septicius has been murdered as well.

Kristeva's ability to tell a story develops here in a way that incorporates the pleasure, and especially the threat, of unconscious drives. The unconscious threatens Delacour's narrative much more than in *The Samurai*, primarily in the form of the death drive and in the male authority figures with which it is connected. In part 2, she is haunted by a "premonition of horror" (82). Initiating the relationship in order to learn more about the murdered girl (92–93), Delacour is surprised to learn that she feels pleasure as well as hate in making love to Vespasian. Her words suggest that such pleasure derives from the death drive, incorporated in the power-hungry doctor:

> I was sure, before, that a drunk scattering ciga-
> rette ashes all over the sheets could never give me an or-
> gasm. But afterward I wasn't sure of anything any-
> more. . . . Haven't you ever heard of the unconscious?
> Disgust has all the power of repressed pleasure. . . . And
> the more ashamed I was, the more pleasure I felt. In the
> midst of a nevertheless delightful frenzy I found myself
> hating us both. (92)

Like Septicius, Delacour feels overwhelmed by the voice of ugliness and brutality that is Santa Varvara and will eventually become a wolf herself for a time. Unable to articulate the next episode of her tale (106), her life as a writer is at risk. Here and for example in the following description of the child's riding the sledge in the snow, Kristeva opposes the wolves, associated with aggression and the death instinct, to the mother, linked with nurturing and writing as a life-affirming practice.

In the conclusion, "Capriccio," Delacour's love for Septicius and for his soul mate and hers, her father, warms the cold, hate-filled world of Santa Varvara. The loss of the Old Man reawakens the loss of her father, childhood memories of tender moments on her sledge and at the beach, and ultimately creates a linkage to the lost mother. Like the fetus within the mother, inside the sled, she "snuggles down" and hears her father's and Septicius's words with difficulty. Telling the story of Septicius leads to a reversal of the roles of parent and child. Delacour relives moments of pleasure and anguish with her father and Septicius and, in writing these memo-ries, becomes more adult. She explains, for example, that the im-ages experienced as a child in the snow persist as "fragments as finely carved as frost" (160). The "sensation of winter written into my infant cells . . . makes its way, through words, into my memory and my dreams, dropping icy flakes into the warm bed" (161). The frost and icy flakes, a replacement for the hot ashes the deadly Vespasian had scattered on her breast and bed, are a metaphor for the writer she has become and for the deathly tale she is telling about her father, the Old Man, and the wolves.

The ending itself is ambiguous. She returns to the security and calm of her Latin quarter apartment even as the unconscious unleashes further pain and aggression. She has become a female wolf (183). Amy B. Jones describes a collapse of Delacour's will in the ambiguous conclusion.[4] Michael Wood sees the ending as reactionary. For him, the novel is nostalgic for a world without evil and the Old Man cannot tolerate the possibility of his own implication in the transformation brought about by the wolves.[5] While it is true that Septicius dies in part because he suffers from recognizing the evil within himself, Kristeva is not primarily nostalgic for a world free of evil, as Wood believes. On the contrary, throughout the novel, as I have shown, she depicts characters who recognize the evil and good within themselves and who struggle to live ethically despite their contradictory behavior. Kristeva herself distinguishes her position from nostalgia and reaction in an interview with Bernard Sichère on this novel.[6]

The Old Man and the Wolves ends with Delacour's dilemma, not with Septicius's inability to cope with evil. While she claims to pursue the political project that is Kristeva's own, to reveal the crimes of the "wolves," that is, the various forms of violence they represent including the death drive and sexist practices, at the same time, Delacour allows herself to become bogged down with unanswerable questions: Will she write this story? Will she succeed in conveying the meaning of the Old Man's life, a life inseparable from her father's and her own? Her closing words imply that she will continue resisting the wolves even though, like Bérenger in Ionesco's *Rhinocéros*, she has been tainted by the presence of the beasts, "Expect no quarter. I hate the wolves and now I've got their measure" (182). The implied reference to Ionesco indicates that, for Kristeva, one must resist the psychic formations underlying capitalism's violence and cruel policies no less than those supporting fascism (or communism).

Delacour returns to Santa Varvara in *Possession*. The novel opens with her examining a headless corpse. Having come to cover political events for her Parisian newspaper editor once again, she soon learns that her friend Gloria Harrison, a well-known translator, has been murdered and decapitated. Delacour's investigation of the murder constitutes the plot, a blend of detective story or murder mystery and philosophical tale not unlike that of *The Old Man and the Wolves*. Much of her time is spent with Northrop Rilsky, the police chief in charge of the formal investigation, and Larry Smirnoff, the editor of the local paper, each of whom shows a personal interest in the attractive French reporter.

As is frequently the case when an author develops her narrative skill in later novels, Kristeva's fiction has become less overtly autobiographical here. A few direct links to her life remain: like the Bulgarian author, Delacour is a writer marked by the memory of both her beloved father and by some distasteful associations with the formerly communist Eastern European country where she lived part of her life.

Kristeva's focus in this return to Santa Varvara will be on child and mother rather than on the father, however. Beginning with the psychological formations underlying the relation to children and lovers (first Harrison's and later those of the speech therapist, Pauline Gadeau), Kristeva stages an identification with the maternal/feminine as she relates Delacour's investigation of the murder.

Kristeva's theory underpins both Delacour's and Harrison's lives in ways that, as in *The Old Man*, reveal their confrontation with the threat of the death drive and of the authority figures and social conventions with which it is associated. Delacour identifies with a feminine/maternal figure from the start of this novel: a pull-out bed, for example, her refuge wherever she may be, is "a giantess to shelter, reassure, or ultimately swallow her" (22). Delacour sees herself in Gadeau, and principally in Harrison, as she describes the translator's troubling past: the little girl's obsession with the story of a mother who gives her life so that her son may live; her marriage to a painter, Stan Kovak, who becomes indifferent to her her affair with a lover, Michael Fish, an opportunist primarily interested in her money and body, in that order, and, especially, the birth of her deaf child Jerry, who consumes most of her energy and time. Kristeva writes, "Just like you and me, Gloria is looking for something light—it doesn't matter whether it's fast or slow, noxious or harmless. Take your pick, draw the curtains, zap from one channel to another! Politics, metaphysics, aesthetics, aerobics, robotics—anything but *it*. No proud scars, please; no pale dignities or clammy palms clutching the hand of a child who's different and gives you the impression, the false impression, that he holds the entire universe in an invisible, unshed tear" (57). In this passage, Delacour consciously links her suffering to Harrison's as she seeks relief from the difficult and sometimes thankless task of subordinating oneself to another person.

Part 1, "A Beheading," sets in motion not only Delacour's identification with the feminine and with Harrison as they cope with a menacing social contract and death drive, but also other vital components of Kristeva's theory. Harrison's reliance on Jerry's needs in order to live in the linguistic forms she teaches him is, in some ways, like Delacour's dependency on Harrison, especially in order to write. The story of the murder becomes the story of Delacour's efforts, often recounted in the first person, to become a mature writer with the Harrison tale serving as food for thought and growth. Delacour lives alternately as an adult writer/amateur detective and as a child: she enjoys the velvety voice of her mother (35) as she contemplates Stan's painting and seeks the approval of her father (40) while she considers whether to pursue detective work and journalism.

Delacour and Harrison's familial dramas are woven into the fabric of Santa Varvara as an Eastern European city wallowing in corruption after the fall of the Soviet Union and the Berlin Wall. Delacour's Parisian newspaper, *Evénements*, sends her there to cover human rights violations and other political events. She goes back again a year and a half later in the novel's conclusion ostensibly to investigate the smuggling of plutonium. Smirnoff and Rilsky believe it is the society itself and especially its corrupt politicians who are indirectly responsible for Harrison's death. In a not-so-hidden critique of Western priorities, including government policies, the journalist and policeman describe how the politicians have seized control of the property of the mental institutions, displaced the patients, and created lucrative tourist attractions. The country's neglect of the mentally ill, according to Smirnoff and Rilsky, has apparently allowed two escaped inmates to decapitate Harrison's dead body. Her murder and beheading come to represent Santa Varvara and its problems, including the legacy of an intolerant regime and its ill-planned transition to capitalism, as Delacour's and Smirnoff's articles in the French press make clear. The speculations concerning the murder enable Kristeva to point the finger both at the Western powers, the primary example being the United States, and at the formerly communist countries of Eastern Europe like her own Bulgaria.

Kristeva is also pointing the finger at the police captain and editor. In the context of the novel and of the rest of Kristeva's work, their ineffective condemnation of "society" and its "corrupt politicians" represents a hackneyed, dead-end analysis and an inability to see the psychological patterns of domination underlying and linking Harrison's murder and Santa Varvara's problems as a city, for instance, the displaced mental patients. Rilsky's and Smirnoff's bickering is not unlike that of the Santa Varvarans described earlier in *The Old Man* who, when not watching television, fight among themselves.

Part 2 of *Possessions*, "Virtual Crime," reveals the secret of Harrison's decapitation and the depth of Delacour's ethical position as detective/writer. A third familial drama unfolds as Delacour learns about Gadeau's painful past. Her childhood and teenage years were marked by a troubled relationship to her mother and by a close bond to a younger brother Aimeric. Delacour describes Gadeau and Aimeric's swimming together on the Brittany coast as a sensual and tender activity combining sibling, mother–child, and romantic affection. Just twenty-two and emotionally dependent on Aimeric, Gadeau is ill equipped to deal with her brother's drowning. She suffers a mental breakdown soon after the death, sees a psychotherapist, takes antidepressants, spends time in a mental institution, and undergoes electroshock treatments. When she takes on the job of Jerry's speech therapist, she becomes dependent once again, this time on the boy who replaces Aimeric in her life.

Gadeau is convinced that Harrison is a bad mother who threatens Jerry's well-being with, for example, periodic outbursts of temper. When Gadeau discovers Harrison's corpse, Delacour surmises, the speech therapist is particularly distraught over the fact that the mother had changed her will to give half of her wealth to Michael Fish instead of Jerry. As Delacour reconstructs the crime, it is probable that Gadeau, blinded by years of suffering and deluded into thinking she is acting in Jerry's best interests, calmly attacks Harrison, cutting off her head, placing it in a plastic bag, and disposing of it in a garbage can en route to Easter vacation in the countryside with the young man.

From early on in *Possessions*, Delacour is examining her own psychic life while narrating that of the other characters. She tells her story in part out of an ethical impulse to defend Harrison and herself who arouse resentment and even hate in others because they are successful women writers who are capable of intense passion as well as strong maternal love. Delacour, we learn halfway through the novel, is recovering from her own difficult relationship to a man and to a child, the fetus she had to abort some years before because of complications during pregnancy. As in *The Samurai* in which she tries to interpret the nightmare of her father's decapitation (139), the journalist struggles to understand a recent dream in which the Italian painter Artemesia Gentileschi depicts the biblical Judith cutting off King Holofernes's head by plunging her sword into his mouth. A third-person omniscient voice, folded into Delacour's "I" narrator, describes the attack as "a kind of endless rape" (128). In the context of the problematic relations between the sexes in this novel (Harrison and Stan, Harrison and Michael, Delacour and her lover) and in *The Old Man* (Alba and Vespasian), the dreams portray Delacour's violent reaction to the male figures with whom she chooses to spend her time, despite the fact that they in part control her life, especially her sexual activity. Trying to come to grips with the dream in *Possessions* and to analyze the experience of sexual pleasure, the narrator says:

No, sex had never been rape for Stephanie, whatever her feminist friends might claim in the name of humanity or femininity. In fact that was why she had had to stop seeing them. It was never rape. Never. On the contrary, it was secret intoxication, smooth as velvet. A heart filled with blood in the body of a nun. Flowers open to the sky in a Georgia O'Keeffe painting. Scents made tangible in the pages of Colette. Stephanie could recognize in other people's work the nameless pleasure that men gave *her*. And that she liked to keep hidden and apart. (129–30)

Later, the narrator says, "In fact, there had been a sort of rape" (131). She acknowledges the desire for sex with a man in the first quotation ("intoxication . . . smooth as velvet . . . a heart filled with blood . . . flowers open . . . scents made tangible . . . pleasure) at the same time that she conceals the desire. It must be "secret," "in the body of a nun," "nameless," "hidden," and "apart." Kristeva implies that pleasure, with its feminine associations ('flowers open") is necessarily subject to a kind of denial of the subject, to judgment, repression, and condemnation frequently connected to the masculine ("a sort of rape"). In other words, it is threatened and ultimately connected to death.

Kristeva practices a complex feminist politics in the episodes in *Possessions* described above and hereafter. The focus is on positive figures who are biologically female whereas in episodes described earlier in *The Old Man* the focus is on the maternal as a social construction or set of associations in a man or woman. In *Possessions*, Delacour makes clear that her efforts to find Harrison's murderer are part of a larger project to defend successful women who are under attack (10–11). Describing Delacour's attitude toward heterosexual sex, Kristeva uses masculine and feminine as biological essences to the degree that the episode focuses on a woman having sex with a man. The principal focus of Kristeva's writing viewed as a whole, however, is on the psychological associations made with the sexes that are not biologically determined. Thus, the discussion

of heterosexual lovemaking draws on socially constructed psychological links that are gendered ("flowers open," "a sort of rape").
Gadeau, to take a different example from *Possessions,* is a woman but
most frequently personifies the masculine and the death drive.

In the last few pages of *Possessions,* Delacour pays a visit to
Jerry and reflects on a woman's relationship to a child—Harrison's,
Gadeau's, and, indirectly, her own. The figure of Gadeau dominates the visit to Jerry: like Freud's censor on the threshold, she
stands in the doorway of Harrison's study as Delacour feels a rush
of love for the boy. Delacour's feeling recalls that of his mother
and of Gadeau with important differences. While Harrison's con-
sumed all her energy, Gadeau's was a deadly ritual of mourning
that led to the beheading. What, the novel implicitly asks, is the
precise nature of Delacour's love for Jerry? Interrupted by Captain
Rilsky's phone call inviting her to a Mozart concert, Delacour escapes from her difficult reflections for a while, just as she seeks so-
lace in her Parisian apartment at the end of both *Possessions* and
The Old Man and the Wolves. She will, however, not avoid the pain
of Harrison's murder and beheading, and by implication, the suffering deriving in part from her own abortion. The final lines of
the novel reveal that, if Delacour has decided not to continue her
efforts to convince Rilsky of Gadeau's crime, she *will* confront the
pain of this act without succumbing to the death drive. That is, in
her writing and in her own relationships, she will continue to
study Gadeau's crime and its implications for understanding a
woman's love for a child and lover. Paris, described with affection
in all three of Kristeva's novels, is not an escape but the place for
Delacour to come to grips with her loss—here, her lost lover and
baby—relived in that of the speech therapist, "Pauline's demon already possessed Ms. Delacour, and it was in this apparently indifferent but secretly passionate guise that he was preparing to
descend on the logical landscape of Paris" (211).

Like the victim in this tale, Delacour, the narrator implies, has
"trained herself to love" and to be more or less "incapable of hate"
(210). She is different from Gadeau who, having never recovered
emotionally from her brother's death, becomes a machine that

coldly disposes of everything she sees as an impediment to Jerry's happiness, including his mother's head. Delacour is also unlike the computer that mechanically reproduces Picassos as Jerry has programmed it to do. She is a kind of artist whose task is not automatic. Delacour strives to live with pleasure and purpose while remaining subject to the threat of male authority. She s committed to helping others do so as well—Jerry, for example, in the ending—and to defend this ethics in her writing, the principal example of which is arguably *Possessions*.

Kristeva's novels, especially *The Old Man and the Wolves* and *Possessions*, stand on their own and, at the same time, embody the most useful developments of her theory. The protagonist's quest for pleasure and the feminine, her identification with others, including mother and father figures, the reversals in the roles of child and parent, the threatening confrontation with pain and death set in a specific historical environment, the political commitment to helping others both directly and in writing, are components of both her theory and fiction. Together, they bring a feminist, historical perspective to bear on life at the close of the twentieth-century, including both its multiple manifestations of hate and its potential for love.

Like the protagonists of *The Old Man* and *Possessions*, the women writers whom Kristeva studies in *Feminine Genius*[7]—Hannah Arendt, Melanie Klein, and Colette—to varying degrees identify with the feminine and are politically active, historically informed, and ultimately successful in their struggles to write influential books that, at the same time, enable them to overcome bouts of depression and masochism. Creatively engaged in the world in the sense that their writing reconfigures love and political relations, they shape an environment open to a degree of change and freedom for the individual.

These works demonstrate Kristeva's feminist politics: she examines the category of "the feminine," revealing and subverting domination built in part on gender. In *Life: Hannah Arendt, or Action as Birth and Estrangement*, Kristeva demonstrates how, for Arendt, totalitarianism destroys the individual in that it damages affect and the political as constructive manifestations of an agent seeking a public existence.[8] In her writing, Arendt attempts to rebuild a political life through links discovered by memory (in part, of the miracle of birth) in an effort to create a social identity for herself. *Madness: Melanie Klein, or Matricide as Pain and Creativity* focuses on Klein's theory of the infant's struggle with melancholia and the death drive in response to being invaded and later abandoned by the mother.[9] Klein discovers a primitive form of constructive thought in the infant's earliest life in the relation to the mother's breast, a relation vital to the individual's later sense of self. The search for the lost object that is the mother brings on a depression that is stimulating, creative, and ultimately, revolutionary. In a remarkable parallel to Klein's work, Colette's *L'Enfant et les Sortilèges, The Infant and Enchantment,* a libretto written for Ravel's music, has the infant at its center and depicts the difficulties faced in separating from the mother.[10]

From Kristeva's perspective in *Colette,* a focus on the mother rather than on the infant is more usual in her work. Colette initially turns to writing partly as a reaction to the pain of heterosexuality as she replays her relationships to her two husbands and especially to the suffering brought on by separating from her mother. One of the first to depict heterosexual love's tendency to shape woman into an object, Colette also examines a variety of other stages women frequently experience in an intimate relation with a man: pleasure without a partner, and jealousy of, and desire for, the rival. Some of her best writing describes the metamorphoses she undergoes as a bisexual woman.

Like Delacour in Kristeva's novels, Colette achieves semiautonomy as a writer, living with pleasure and purpose while remaining subject to the threat of male authority, for instance, in *Tendrils of the Vine* (*Les Vrilles de la vigne,* 1908).[11] Kristeva places Colette and, in particular, this collection of short, passionate essays, at the center of Western erotic literature invented by women with roots in the Sulamite female narrator of the biblical *Song of Songs* (see Kristeva's *Colette,* 328). Colette's contribution lies in her imagining sexuality as a diverse spectrum that, while marked to some degree by pain, is ultimately a positive construction. Kristeva mentions Marguerite Yourcenar, Marguerite Duras, and Natalie Sarraute among the major twentieth-century figures who write in Colette's wake. In *Tendrils of the Vine*, a nightingale/artist sings the suffering and fear aroused by a lesbian love. With a keen sense of the significant psychological and literary discoveries of the West (see her analysis of Bakhtin and DeLaSale discussed earlier), Kristeva indicates that Colette expresses such a love at the time (in fact, twenty-three years earlier) that Freud described woman's psyche as more frequently bisexual than man's (see *Colette* and Freud's *Female Sexuality*[12]). Kristeva also reveals that, like Proust, Colette is able to portray with great depth the latency stage of early adolescence in which both joy and anxiety dominate the psyche as its sexual orientation matures, for example, in the episode "The Wedding" in *My Mother's House* (*La Maison de Claudine*, 1922).[13]

Kristeva sees Colette's work as a whole, including *Tendrils* and *My Mother's House*, growing out of her response to the mother. From Kristeva's perspective, Colette is one of the few writers, female or male, to explore the experience of motherhood, not as a primarily biological or potentially reactionary process, but as a sociopsychic formation supporting a child or a lover. Virginia Woolf is another important example in England a few years later. Nurturing another person, child or adult, provides the basis for a feminist position in Kristeva and in Colette. In Kristeva, this position begins with an identification with the maternal and effectively undercuts domination in both private and public life to the degree that the relation to the other is supportive, and, especially in the case of a lover, reciprocal. While she has rejected the feminist label, like her protagonist, Delacour (as discussed earlier), and has called attention to the potentially reactionary role of motherhood elsewhere, Kristeva's thought is feminist in the broad sense that her work examines the status of the category of woman, contributes to knowledge production and undercuts damaging, hierarchical structures. In her chapter "A Little Politics Nevertheless" in *Colette*, she states "We have a chance of recovering our freedoms on condition that we *represent* ourselves as vagabond or in shackles [referring to two of Colette's book titles]. Freedom being, by definition, what is principally at stake in politics, which is to say that representing the passions—what we call 'the imaginary'—is in no way a setting without significance but *an integral part of politics*" (474).

Like other Modernist, feminist texts including, for example, Woolf's *Mrs. Dalloway*, *Tendrils* has a structure different from the linear time sequence of much realistic narrative (see chapter 4 of this volume). Such "well made" prose creates the illusion of a rational order in which, for instance, discontinuities and the unconscious are minimized. In *Tendrils*, a cyclical pattern emerges, appropriate in these twenty-one short, diverse chapters replaying three themes: homosexual love, male psychology, and, more covertly, the figure of the mother, traditionally associated with the cycles of reproduction.[14] Love unfolds in essays describing a significant other who remains nameless, friends, especially Valentine, and pets, cats and dogs for whom the narrator feels affection to the point of identifying with them. While Colette's narrator is at various times melancholy, fearful, lyrical, cynical, or masochistic, the overall tone and content of the collection is reflective and constructive.

In her best and most characteristic work, as Kristeva's analysis of *Tendrils* and the following discussion of *My Mother's House* show, Colette focuses on the mother as a source of bodily and psychic memories of pleasure and pain. Growing out of her rapport with Sido, her own mother, and the homosexual component implicit in it, Colette's portrait of the mother is complex: she is typically a powerful, joyful figure if, at times, threatened by both the masculine and a certain tendency bordering on, but ultimately steering clear of, masochism. The first poses the risk of domination by an exterior force, embodied in Colette's first husband, the infamous Willy, and associated with the phallus and the second, by a component of the subject herself, in part made abject as a result of domination by the masculine.

Colette writes *My Mother's House*, like *Tendrils of the Vine* and much of her work, in brief chapters often only four pages long, describing everyday events. Using an apparently simple representation of ordinary life—in the case of this autobiographical novel, of her mother, from her marriage to "the Savage" until her feisty old age—

she expresses desire for the maternal as a visceral, homosexual experience, and, in light of Kristeva's theory, as a feminist politics. Colette reconstructs her mother's life without explicit focus on a plot building to a central climax in the mode of the nineteenth-century masters of Realism. Instead, *My Mother's House* is a series of "minor," implicit discoveries about her mother. Colette takes one of the most stereotypical of female icons, the home, and depicts it in the seemingly unrelated events that occur in a Burgundian village. The home is primarily an environment that the young daughter, Colette, comes to recognize as the center of her being as she matures (25). Colette gives resonance to parallel episodes revealing a vibrant, desirable mother figure. *My Mother's House* introduces the home as a place that was alive because of the woman inside it but, in a masochistic move that will be repeated later, as a world of which the narrator feels she has "ceased to be worthy" (6). One of the final sections on the narrator's daughter's life highlights the sensual girl—primarily the daughter, but also the mother—that she is no longer, ostensibly because of the cliché that she has grown up to be a conventional adult. In the context of the book and, for example, the earlier statement about unworthiness, the daughter is no longer the sensual girl because, in a final instance of Colette's struggle with masochism, the narrator becomes self-destructive and feels that a break has occurred with what the mother has come to represent by the text's end (138–141).

From the beginning, Colette expresses desire for a lost mother in Sido, in her daughter, and ultimately, in herself. The narrator who is at first Sido's daughter, Colette, shifts between and within chapters to the degree that one is unsure who precisely is speaking: she is at times a third-person omniscient narrator, at times, a daughter who has become the mother herself. It is clear that the narrator desires the mother, that the mother and daughter-become-mother were one in a close homosexual relationship in which body and spirit flourish in a home filled with, for example, their beloved cats, dogs, and books.

The shifting narrative voice provides the distance, enabling one to become aware of this desire for the union between mother and daughter and of the fact that the daughter of the first pages develops into the mother of later episodes in a new relationship between Colette and her own daughter, Minet-Chéri/Bel Gazou. The most significant mother figure in this work is the narrator herself, whose writing successfully enacts a union with the daughter and connects the apparently unrelated episodes, some of which stage a masochistic conflict or melodrama in which masculine authority oppresses her.

Virginia Best calls attention to the way in which the mother's desire for the daughter (the desire to be the daughter's love object) is part of an inherited chain linking generations of women and informing her subjectivity.[15] While Best focuses on Duras's *The Lover* (*L'Amant*), with some reference to Emma Wilson's reading of Cixous's theories of the feminine erotic, the passage is part of a larger discussion including Kristeva and Colette that is relevant to the question of essentialism in Kristeva. As I read Best's analysis, in both Kristeva and Colette, writing creates an individual sense of self, that is, it confers a degree of autonomy, even as it celebrates a joyful entry into a kind of pantheistic "feminine," a world with multiple cosmic links where individuals and the sexes are not bound to the hierarchies and biology in which they may suffer. While Best's commentary (and Kristeva and Colette's texts) may appear biologist/essentialist, they are not to the extent that biology is one element, and not a determining one, in establishing sexual identity, as I have argued throughout this book.

At the heart of the mother figures is sensual pleasure. Colette, like Sido, is powerful because of her joy in living, despite the twin specters of masochism or of masculine authority threatening her from within or without. She exercises considerable authority in the home, assuming at times a masculine role that, in this case, is not threatening. She uses it, for example, to prevent alcohol abuse in the episode in which, once she finds out that drinking too much wine is responsible for her nine-year-old daughter's sleep, she forbids Colette to accompany her father on his trips to give political/moral talks in area cafés. The text uses sight to describe two instances of Sido's zest for life: her eye contact with the men she meets—a habit echoing Flaubert's young Madame Bovary—and her "curiosity [which] led her to seek [evil] out, and to consider it, jumbled up with good, with wondering eyes" (36). A third example occurs in her old age when she rises early to saw wood before others could prevent her from taking on this vigorous work (in a chapter appropriately entitled "My Mother and the Forbidden Fruit," 127–30).

Colette inherits the capacity for physical pleasures, including not only the wine I have already mentioned, but also her passionate identification with her pets, dogs and cats. She identifies, too, with the awakening of the world in spring—a description harkening back, on a smaller scale, to the one in Thoreau's *Walden*, equally evocative in its recall of earlier springs and earlier selves, especially those solidified in Transcendentalist language. Like Thoreau, Colette creates an individual sense of self in writing while at the same time celebrating her immersion in nature, or more accurately, her bursting forth like a flower in the spring (Kristeva recognizes the key metaphor of bursting forth or "*éclosion*," in her work), creating multiple links with the universe. In *My Mother's House*, Colette's capacity for pleasure manifests itself especially in her memories of sisters, both Sido's half sister from Martinique, and Colette's own half sister, Juliette.

Colette recalls Sido's half sister in the form of a brief reverie on chocolate, flowers, and cats emerging in the episode "'My Father's Daughter.'" Like Juliette, Colette's half sister, in a later chapter that reverses the time sequence and has the more significant memory grow out of the earlier one, Sido's half sister has an ephemeral, miraculous, and exotic quality. Listening to her mother's tale about the half sister, born in Martinique to her African-Caribbean, chocolate-maker father, the narrator smells the chocolate bricks and sees the delicate flowers imprinted in the chocolate by cats' paws passing through the terrace where the bricks are cooling. Despite hygiene concerns that might inhibit some contemporary readers, the reverie functions as an imaginative reconstruction of a precious, synesthetic moment anticipating the more fully developed episode to come. Kristeva's word "*coenesthésies*" (coesthesia), in discussing Colette's work from the Claudine series to Sido (417), is perhaps more appropriate than "synesthesia" for the simultaneous experience of different sensations that retain their respective strengths.

Juliette's exoticism, appearing soon after "'My Father's Daughter,'" in the more complex episode "My Sister with the Long Hair," resides in her Kalmuk or Mongolian appearance, in her obsessive reading that appears to weaken her to the point where she contracts typhoid fever, and, especially, in her extraordinary dark, wavy hair. Colette's description of the hair transforms the physical attribute into a coesthetic and sexual experience. The preface to the description of Juliette talks about the narrator's own prodigious hair and, in a kind of hymn to hair in the tradition of Baudelaire's *La Chevelure* (*The Head of Hair*), asks who will bathe in its waves, describing the hair as a barbarian adornment, smelling of animals, something you touch lovingly "in secret for secret purposes" (69). While twisted and rolled for the public, hair is spread apart in private; if one surprises a woman while she is doing her hair, she will flee as if she were naked; it is only in bed that hair is free, a network of herbs inhabiting the sheets, irritating the skin, and coming into contact with a stray hand. About to introduce Juliette, Colette states that, despite the difficulty encountered in controlling the hair, brief instants of pleasure in the morning or at night when one beholds a shining, savage face framed by the free-falling waves, render meaningless the aversion for long hair expressed earlier (70).

The description of Juliette, like the phrase that Colette uses to refer to her and to title the chapter, highlights her hair and, in Kristeva's theory, a maternal/semiotic threatened by but also somewhat complicit with the paternal/symbolic. It invades her, covering the body completely, coiling around her wrist like a snake. Overwhelming both Juliette and the half sister who is responsible for combing and brushing it, Sido calls it "un mal inguérissable" (an incurable evil) (1014; in the French version). The sexual associations continue in the account of the narrator's feelings of ennui, pride, and desire as she enters the older sister's room brimming with all of its "inaccessible wonders" (72). Juliette is obsessed with her reading and barely responds to her sister or Sido and, equally significant, in a patriarchal, largely heterosexual world where the incest taboo persists (one recalls that Colette's biography nevertheless documents relations with her stepson), the narrator's desires are repressed ("ma convoitise domptée" [my covetousness overcome]; 1014–16; in the French version). A large lock of thick, shining hair emerges one final time in the conclusion of the chapter as the ironically penislike coil throbbing with life returns to block the face of the delirious Juliette. Her mother hides her own face, overcome with shame, ostensibly because Juliette, a kind of black sheep in the family, is hallucinating, calling her mother "Catulle Mendès," the author she has been reading.

In relating the episodes on the sisters and, more generally, the wide variety of episodes making up *My Mother's House*, the shifting, difficult-to-identify narrator is born into the feminine, a feminine frequently threatened by the masculine, and at times, bordering on masochism. Colette intersperses the chapters with a recurring pattern of masculist behavior or death. Early in the book, a series of marriages, for example, are described as "abductions." The "Savage" arranges the marriage to the young Sido, plucked from her comfortable bohemian home in Belgium to find herself depressed in an isolated country manor in Burgundy, France (Montigny). In a rare statement directly confronting patriarchal authority, albeit with some affection ("loving suspicion"; 29), Sido will later suggest to her husband that even her second, happier marriage to him was a kind of "abduction," the title of the chapter dealing with Sido's recurrent nightmares and containing her confrontational statement, "And after all, you, what have you to do with me? You aren't even a relation!" (28). After Juliette marries and leaves her bed to her sister, Colette's mother dreams that her younger daughter was kidnapped. In the same chapter, Colette describes her fascination with the painting entitled *The Abduction*, hanging by her old bedroom adjoining her mother's. The painting depicts a wealthy man picking up a young woman, tossed back with her legs framed by a swirl of skirts, her mouth dropping open. In the chapter's conclusion, Colette screams, "Mother! Come quick! I've been abducted" (29) when, after Sido had carried her back to her old bedroom, the daughter awakens to find herself in unfamiliar surroundings.

Remarkable for its emotional intensity and its nuanced narration of a lovely June wedding that degenerates into a mediocre and ultimately deathlike consummation, the chapter inserted just before the Juliette episode, recounts Colette's eagerness at puberty to participate as bridesmaid in the marriage of a servant, Adrienne. Excited by the love-stricken Adrienne's transformation into a happy coquette primping at the mirror, Colette throws herself joyfully into the event, her hair waved, enjoying the four-course meal. In the end, however, having eaten and drunk too much, she finds that not only does her girlfriend's sweaty arm touching her skin bother her, but also she becomes anxious and fearful, hearing of the sexual escapades of the other young people. The lit window of the newlyweds' bedroom displays a huge armoire that, with the low ceiling, leaves little space for the narrow, high bed. The sickening smell of roses and chamomile associated with funerals, contaminates the confined, oppressive space, "this stifling little tomb" (68) and descends to the garden where her friend and Colette pass. She panics at the sudden thought of the married couple's "dark struggle" ("cette lutte obscure"; 1012; in the French version) in the conclusion of "The Wedding." The little girl still strong in her, she screams, "I want to go home to mother" (68) in a version of the earlier cry in "The Abduction."

Kristeva's theory helps show how Colette's writing overcomes the threat of patriarchal authority, steers clear of the dangers of masochism, and is, for the most part, politically and historically informed. The instances of death or patriarchal oppression are not isolated. They include also Colette's brother's morbid game in the garden where he creates cardboard tombstones (for the local dead) and the young, graceful actor who, arriving with his troupe to perform in the town, is chased out by the authoritarian and homophobic *châtelain*. The latter had returned from a trip to find the actor doing embroidery with a delighted citizenry, both male and female.

Thus, *My Mother's House* constitutes a celebration of the feminine despite the frequent risks: with this work, Colette proves herself to be, precisely, worthy of her mother's "world," that is, somewhat ironically, still a creative little girl, contrary to the narrator's autopunitive statements. The final words speak of her daughter rediscovering the melody of an imaginary song, "fragile as a strand of hair or a blade of grass" ("fine comme un cheveu, fine comme une herbe"; 1084; in the French version). Kaja Silverman's book *The Acoustic Mirror: The Female Voice in Psychoanalysis and Cinema* suggests the relevance of Kristeva's theory to Colette's work, especially to this episode. As her title indicates, Silverman explains how Kristeva elaborates a theory of the mother's voice that the child hears and in which she or he discovers a sense of identity. *The Acoustic Mirror* is ultimately wrong in its statement that Kristeva's notion of the feminine is essentialist and aligns woman with nature. On the contrary, as this chapter demonstrates, the feminine is not primarily a biological category in Kristeva but rather a psychosocial set of associations connected to individuals who are biologically male or female. Silverman's book nevertheless contains an excellent close reading of her "Place Names" and "Motherhood According to Giovanni Bellini," demonstrating that the theorist's concept of the maternal voice "functions in some very profound way as the libidinal base for feminism."[16]

Kristeva's psychoanalytic perspective helps one see the bipolar categories of maternal and paternal in Colette as interwoven associations that shape but do not bind identity. *My Mother's House* is both politically and historically informed, chronicling provincial France in the twenties, with politics and social history evident in the events dealing directly and less directly with sexuality. From Kristeva's point of view, Colette offers an imaginative response to the problem of seemingly inevitable aggression, with the war between the sexes not unrelated to that which exists in the military.

In a passage of *Colette* paralleling the examination of Céline's problematic attitude to the Nazis (see the discussion of *Powers of Horror* in chapter 5 of this volume), Kristeva discusses the most troubling component of Colette's politics, her failure to understand World War II and to condemn fascism. Married to a Jew,

Maurice Goudeket (who is arrested by the Nazis in 1941), and perhaps influenced by her daughter from her earlier marriage, Colette De Jouvenal, who becomes an activist and editor for the Resistance, Colette eventually comprehends Hitler's domination and rejects fascism once she has directly experienced it.[17]

Despite the important lapse that Kristeva recognizes, Colette's radical political and historical sense is evident in *My Mother's House* as in much of her writing. Kristeva shows, via the novelist's references and discussion of Balzac, to whom she devoted long hours of reading and four substantial essays, that for Colette psychological formations constituting a monstrous sensuality are the foundation for the middle class's social ambitions and for the disappearing aristocracy's elitist practices as documented by the famous Realist. Kristeva's *Colette* explains that the writer makes her radical politics evident primarily in an effort to liberate psychic formations by representing a monstrous sensuality no less than does Balzac, but normally without the staging of ambition and elitist behavior for which he is wellknown. Thus, for instance, an unusually intense fear and anxiety over heterosexual sex as a form of domination and death underlie the chapter "The Wedding" (discussed earlier) where Colette attends Adrienne's marriage. The historical moment and class distinctions are significant: not unlike many middle-class French of her time and today, Sido, for example, sees the servants as an inferior group that should be kept apart from respectable people and will not accept the Septmance family's invitation, finding Adrienne's request that Colette be bridesmaid "really very awkward" (64). (It is true that Colette's mother's snobbery in this episode is less intense than that of her neighbors: normally quite unconventional for her time, she endures their fingerpointing and refuses to dismiss her pregnant maid. In fact, she remembers her own love of servants' weddings when she was thirteen.) More significantly and not unlike the description of her mother's snobbery in this respect, Colette's implicit critique of heterosexuality in the episode and throughout the text, especially in "My Sister with the Long Hair," demonstrates the novelist's skills as a social historian staging woman's increasing ability to live her sexuality in the early twentieth century. It seems likely that Colette's keen interest in female servants in this episode and elsewhere in the text derives at least in part from the fact that, compared to their middle-class counterparts, the maids are more "liberated," that is, both more active sexually and more mobile socially. Like other members of a new generation of French middle-class women—Simone De Beauvoir being the best-known example—Colette's interest is not shared by her mother.

Diana Fuss's book, *Identification Papers*, provides an illuminating context for a reading of Kristeva's political sense in general and especially in the latter's commentary in *Colette*. Fuss's analysis goes beyond Silverman's in demonstrating psychoanalytic theory's potentially radical politics and, more to the point of the argument I am making, in demonstrating Kristeva's feminist ethics. In an incisive examination of identification—along with desire, arguably the most important concept in Freudian theory, she points out—Fuss makes a compelling argument for psychoanalytic criticism, theory, and fiction as a radical politics using Franz Fanon as an example. She states that identifying with, for example, the feminine, brings with it the entry of the historical/cultural into the subject, presumably because gendered individuals are necessarily situated in time and space. Fuss analyzes a little-known work of Freud, "The Psychogenesis of a Case of Homosexuality in a Woman," and demonstrates the ways in which homosexuality is a social practice, a symbolic association inscribed in representation, sociality, and culture: Freud's patient—not unlike the young Colette in the chapter on the servant's wedding discussed previously—desires women who are socially mobile and who earn their living—an actress, a prostitute, and a teacher—independently of the heterosexual social contract of the time (57–82). Fuss is, however, incorrect to align Kristeva with Freud's "normative" theories of sexual identity and even with his homophobia (59).[18] *Colette* sees the identification with the feminine and its homosexual component as a positive form of desire, while also presenting the identification as a violation of the law.

Moving beyond Freud's notions of "the normal" and of the father of individual pre-history, Kristeva offers a version of psychoanalysis in her novels and recent theory in which formidable female figures spring to life. She shows how Colette's texts in particular enact an identification with a maternal figure in a world charged with the sensual. Kristeva's feminist politics reveals Colette's creation of a sexuality unafraid to have its "scents made tangible in the pages."

✦ Conclusion ✦

I have written this book in part to demonstrate that Kristeva's work on the gendered psychic formations in the West and their influence on sociopolitical stratification contributes significantly to an understanding of many of the most serious conflicts in such countries as the United States and France. A vast array of related personal and political problems such as the psychological impasses faced by many individuals in their efforts to think creatively, mental illness, and even a conflict that appears unrelated to Kristeva's work, such as the Iraq War, can be better understood in its light.

The question of power connects Kristeva's writing to a conflict like the war. In terms of structure, gendered psychic formations shape identifications and power relations first within the family and later and similarly among larger social groups and are a source of interpersonal and international conflicts over whose interests should be served. Diana Fuss, Daniel O'Hara, and Luce Irigaray's works provide a context that shares this conclusion.[1] As Daniel O'Hara, puts it in the lead article in his recent special edition of the *Journal of Modern Literature* on "Global Freud: Psychoanalytic Cultures and Classic Modernism," "Society . . . take(s) the shape and speak(s) the language of the family . . . and of a people" (7). An examination of the process of identification enables one to see how Kristeva's theory helps in understanding personal/familial problems and their connection to contemporary national/international conflicts. I conclude that the study of identification as the process plays itself out in language, inserting the individual into culture and history[2] and coupled with a Marxist-inspired analysis of whose material interests these processes serve, is critical to knowing the contemporary world.

Like Irigaray's writings on sexual difference, this book emphasizes the connections among individual, familial, and national conflicts. Ignoring sexual difference in the name of universal rights leads, for example, to the exploitation of women, and, as Irigaray puts it, to "war as a means of regaining some measure of order" (5). Greater comprehension of sexual difference and of the particular plight of women would be a step toward a safer world for everyone. As Irigaray states, "History might find a more continuous course of development, one less subject to periodic expansions and reductions that defy society's control."[3]

I showed in chapter 1 that Kristeva uncovers an androgynous figure, a mother who plays a fatherly role, in Mallarmé. Reading the unconscious in Mallarmé's poetry, she reveals the gendered hierarchies in Western psychic practices. The poet's relation to his mother is replayed in his writing where he celebrates the pleasures of oral gratification in the glottal stops, rhythms, preciosity, and snobbery of the text. Out of this celebration, Kristeva elaborates the functioning of the semiotic and of the symbolic within a signifying process, concepts that have been found useful by many cultural critics who write, at least to some extent, in her wake, for example, Jacqueline Rose.[4] Kristeva uncovers the ways in which the poems give life to psychic struggles that shape and are to a degree reified or repressed by French capitalist ideology. She demonstrates how Mallarmé's poetry stages psychological conflicts in alternating male and female voices, gendered alternations that are linked to social class differences. On an economic level, the poems allude to the beau monde and its supporting government's exploitation of the working class, including the petite bourgeoisie and peasants.

Kristeva goes beyond Freud and Lacan to give greater emphasis to sexual difference by stressing the female rather than the father. Much of her advance depended on the existential Parisian context of the sixties, which allowed her to modify and openly politicize Freud and Lacan. The Existentialist notion of the fluctuating movements of consciousness or the- *pour soi*—while wrong minded in that it often rejects Freud's discovery of the unconscious—enables Kristeva to modify psychoanalysis in an important way. Like Sartre and DeBeauvoir whose radical influence, I argue, is significantly connected to Kristeva's politics, she launches a critique of the capitalist state's class and gender hierarchies by emphasizing the discontinuous processes in the psyche's movements, in the construction of sexuality, and in the alteration of power relations.

Chapter 1 demonstrates how Kristeva's critique of stratification raises questions about the concepts of author and esthetic unity. For her, the text is a psychic formation and a narrative practice using literary form to explode aesthetic unity. In the course of telling his or her story, the author/subject breaks with the social order as she or he comes into being. I conclude from this chapter that her theories, unlike those of other psychoanalytic theorists—Jeffrey Mehlman, for instance—affirm a heterogeneous text giving voice to a multiple subject and supporting a society bent on radical change. I demonstrate this argument at length in my reading of Kristeva and Proust in chapters 2 and 3.

In Kristeva's theory as I analyze it in those chapters, the psychological takes shape in linguistic and literary forms and possesses a political function. From the point of view embodied in an important collection of Kristeva's work between 1969 and 1977, *Desire in Language A Semiotic Approach to Literature and Art* (1980), Proust's *Remembrance of Things Past* (*A La Recherche du temps perdu*) constitutes a break with the social contract. From its beginnings in a marginal work from the fifteenth century, *Jehan de Saintré*, which Kristeva analyzes in this volume, the Realist novel shapes psychic formations that in turn mold social institutions. Mikhail Bakhtin, the Russian theorist and critic whose work is an important influence on Kristeva's theory, convincingly describes this process, as she demonstrates in another influential chapter in this collection. More recently, Paul Ricoeur has similarly examined the psychic structures enabling the literary text to challenge both linguistic and governmental law.[5]

From a perspective informed by Kristeva's theory, Proust demonstrates how salon society and the French Symbolist movement exploit individuals to construct a delusive and repressive self. Christian and Freudian concepts of love also shape such a self in a Kristevan framework. The relationship to the mother, for example, takes on a sadomasochistic character in a Christian tradition associating love with a sense of evil. Chapter 6 comes to the conclusion that Kristeva's work examines the persistence of such stereotypes in fantasy. Thus, the figure of the masochistic woman appearing in the mother is not primarily the unquestioned stereotype that certain critics of Kristeva claim (Jennifer Stone, for instance).[6] In the context of Kristeva's work, the masochistic woman in Proust underlies Proust's indictment of the beau monde. Chapter 3 reveals Proust's complex and ultimately more positive portrayal of the female figure. His novel embraces her life-enhancing behavior and accepts her "authority" in, for example, the madeleine scene understood in light of *Remembrance* as a whole.

Beyond the fact that Kristeva's theory in *Desire in Language* enables a demonstration of the political stance underlying both Antoine DeLaSale and Proust, the essays contained in this collection also reveal a radical politics in her foregrounding of the two marginalized figures, DeLaSale and Bakhtin. The attention that Kristeva pays to Bakhtin and especially to his notion of dialogism is part of her turn to Eastern models, Russian and Chinese, in thinking through a critique of the symbol of the father and of symbolic language in Western patriarchal psychic formations. A fine analysis of the Russian Futurists, Khlebnikov and Mayakovsky, is part of this critique (originally published in 1974; see *Desire in Language*, 30). It is at about this time, upon her return from China with the *Tel Quel* group, that she writes her controversial book *About Chinese Women*. The elaboration of a psychoanalytic, philosophical, and literary theory in these writings during the seventies helps lay a foundation for her feminism, as I conclude in chapter 5.

Chapter 3 demonstrates that, illuminated by Kristeva's work, Proust enacts the drama of his difficulties in achieving a primary identification with the mother. Using components of her theory, I examine the familial drama that emerges in Proust's creation of two characters, the paleographer Saniette and the house servant Françoise. Proust's critique and subversion of the beau monde is latent in the narrator's identifications with these individuals, frequently described in terms that make clear how remote they are from the male authority figures of turn-of-the century France. From this point of view, *Remembrance* reveals how salon society and, in particular, the Symbolistes reduce women to a commodity, a reduction that is, in part, a defense mechanism against the mother's presence.

Like chapters 2, 3, and 5, chapter 4 shows that Kristeva's work is helpful in understanding French Modernist texts, the psychological formations animating them, and the social structures these formations have in part shaped. Her analyses of Khlebnikov and Mayakovsky (along with Proust in chapter 2 of this volume), and of Céline in chapter 5 (see later) make this clear. Informed by Kristeva's theory, an examination of three other Modernist works—DeBeauvoir's *She Came to Stay* (*L'Invitée*), Renoir's *Rules of the Game* (*La Règle du jeu*), and Truffaut's *Jules and Jim* (*Jules et Jim*)—in chapter 4 uncovers their resistance to the hierarchies structuring sexuality and their critical reference to the collaboration with fascism in 1939 in France. In this sense, these texts are part of Modernism as an intellectual movement responding to the disintegration of values that reached one of its climaxes in World War II.

In chapter 4, I argue that a Kristevan perspective discloses a fundamental similarity in DeBeauvoir, Truffaut, and Renoir in that all three texts examine male/female oppositions, giving rise to conflict and anxiety in a female psyche. From this point of view, the texts tell tragic cautionary tales in which using power in a way that harms others is similar to allowing authority to repress a part of oneself.

Chapter 4 also addresses the problem of essentialism which, along with the notion of the masochistic woman, continues to surface in evaluations of Kristeva's work. I argue that while there is a biological component in her neo-Freudian model (the child's first gendered experience being symbiosis with the mother), the link between authority and the male has roots in the Judeo-Christian tradition, is psychologically constructed, and is not necessarily biological.

One of the conclusions of this chapter and of the book is that Kristeva does not theorize a woman determined by her biology but instead equipped psychologically and linguistically to forge a delicate balance between rebellion and authority, a process that is frequently difficult to achieve or sustain. The protagonists in the three works foregrounded in this chapter, for example, do not fulfill the potential for this balance.

In chapter 5, I show that Kristeva develops a feminist position in *Powers of Horror*, *About Chinese Women*, and *The Samurai* despite her statements critical of certain feminists elsewhere (see *Tales of Love*, 374). This chapter confronts the most controversial components of Kristeva's politics, her writing on Céline and Maoist China. Having decided to write in a more accessible manner,[7] she speaks more directly than in much of her earlier writing about women, Jews, and China. In *Powers of Horror*, she indicates the close relationship between women and Jews to the degree that both primarily represent the underside of official culture, that is, an "impure body," while representing the social order at other times.

My study of *Powers of Horror*, including its theories of child psychology and history of Judeo-Christian religious practices, leads to the conclusion that culture is more significant than nature in Kristeva's understanding of human behavior, of the writer, and especially, of women. A haunting work, this volume analyzes, for instance, Céline's staging of traumatic identity crises in the form of identifications with women (and Jews). The writer (man or woman)—here it becomes clear that Kristeva is not essentialist—must identify with the other gender in order to create. He or she must put on a mask and struggle with the demonic or obverse of the conscious self. The writer confronts woman and, in part because of the confrontation, discovers the means to write well in a process that is both creative and political.

Chapter 5 also concludes that *About Chinese Women* and *The Samurai* are forward looking and realistic in their treatment of Céline and China. I demonstrate that Kristeva's writing in these volumes is historically informed and that contentions that it is nostalgic or utopian are invalid, while acknowledging that these two books lack the tension and tragic intensity of her best writing, including *Powers of Horror*.

In *Tales of Love, In the Beginning Was Love*, and *Black Sun*, both mother and father are life-giving figures in a psychoanalytic theory that increasingly gives greater emphasis to sexual difference and to the maternal. *Tales of Love* studies the history of love in the West and demonstrates that Judaic and classical love demand that the subject desire an object that can only be possessed through a separation from the body and from the mother whom the body represents.

In this volume, Kristeva reveals how certain writers, Bernard De Clairvaux, for instance, are able to go beyond the orthodox conception of love. Without idealizing, her analysis of Clairvaux, the case histories of her patients, and the autobiographical chapters theorize both mother and father as life-affirming figures who frequently intervene to enable a partial autonomy.

In one of the best-known examples of such writing in *Tales of Love*, "Stabat Mater," a kind of prose poem, Kristeva invents a rhetoric that stages a mother's break with the dominating discourse of love. Abstract and monolithic, the discourse threatens to deny the body's presence in her words. Thus, the beginning of a radical political practice consists in affirming physical experience and in achieving a tentative independence within oneself.

In the Beginning Was Love uses Kristeva's experience in responding to an invitation to speak at a Catholic school in order to demonstrate how one may risk and recover a sense of independence. Including autobiography, case histories of her patients, and an examination of Catholicism, she examines psychoanalysis as a therapeutic method that can help one move closer to an identification with a loving father. *Black Sun* focuses on what may arguably be the most difficult moment in regaining a degree of autonomy: the woman (or the man who cultivates the feminine component of his psyche) separates from the mother and identifies with an imaginary, loving father.

Among Kristeva's more recent books, the two novels *The Old Man and the Wolves* and *Possessions* and the trilogy *Feminine Genius* unleash the death drive to an extent that arguably makes these texts among her most compelling. The male is increasingly depicted as a threat to writing; it is only with the greatest difficulty that the mother enables the creative process. In *Possessions*, for instance, the narrator/journalist, Stephanie Delacour, identifies with the mother in the form of the murdered translator, Gloria Harrison, whose life and death feed Delacour's efforts to narrate and to complete articles for the Parisian newspaper for which she works. In this case, using the imagination to recreate another person becomes a strategy for having that person sustain oneself. Kristeva's theory underpins both Delacour's and Harrison's lives in ways that, as in *The Old Man*, reveal their confrontation with the threat of the death drive and of the authority figures and social conventions with which it is associated. The final pages of *Possessions* ask what the precise nature of a mother's love for a child is (Delacour's love for Jerry) and reveal that the protagonist will confront the pain experienced in loving a child or lover without succumbing to the death impulse.

From Kristeva's perspective in *Feminine Genius* and *Words: Colette, or the World as Blood and Flesh*, some of Colette's best writing describes the metamorphoses she undergoes as a bisexual woman at times besieged by masculine authority or the death drive. She focuses on the mother as an entity growing out of the author's rapport with Sido, her own mother, and its lesbian associations. Informed by Kristeva's theory, I conclude that Colette expresses desire for the maternal as an intensely sensual experience that is also an indirect feminist politics.

Colette's writing manages to both invent a partial autonomy and inaugurate a pantheistic "feminine" for the subject. Such writing imaginatively connects both sexes to a cosmos in which satisfaction replaces the suffering imposed by gendered hierarchies.[8] In light of Kristeva's book, I come to the conclusion that Colette stages an implicit critique of heterosexuality and demonstrates woman's increasing ability to live her bisexuality.

Like that of Diana Fuss, who explains how identification with the feminine brings with it the subject's historical/cultural existence, Kaya Silverman's work contributes to an understanding of Kristeva's feminist ethics. I show that, while her charge of essentialism is unwarranted, Silverman brings clarity to Kristeva's idea of the mother's voice as an integral part of the child's pleasure and of a feminist perspective. As my book concludes from its examination of *Words: Colette, or the World as Blood and Flesh*, and of Colette's own writing, Kristeva, like the woman she analyzes, struggles with and overcomes the threat of both patriarchal domination and masochism.

Kristeva's work, politically and historically informed, contributes to an understanding of conflict in individuals and groups including families, schools, churches, the military, and the state. Her writing enables if not a redistribution of power and a resolution of such conflicts, at least a degree of progression beyond them. As Kristeva has written in a passage that concisely connects language and politics, "Freedom being, by definition, what is most at stake in politics, one could say, in other words, that the representation of the passions—what is called *"the Imaginary"*—is by no means a trivial background, but *an integral part of politics*."[9]

❧ Notes ❧

1. The Eruption of Conflict

1. *Revolution in Poetic Language*, trans. Margaret Waller (New York: Columbia University Press, 1984). Trans. of *La Révolution du langage poétique* (Paris: Editions du Seuil, 1974). The French version, submitted in partial fulfillment of the requirements for her *doctorat*, is two-thirds longer than the portion translated into English.

2. See, for example, Jacqueline Rose's description of this debate in "Julia Kristeva—Take Two," in *Sexuality in the Field of Vision* (London: Verso, 1986), 151-60.

3. See Paul Ricoeur, "The Question of Proof in Freud's Psychoanalytic Writings," in *The Philosophy of Paul Ricoeur: An Anthology of His Works* (Boston: Beacon Press, 1978), originally published in 1977, 197-98.

4. See *Tales of Love*, trans. Leon S. Roudiez (New York: Columbia University Press, 1987), 242-43.

5. Kelly Oliver uses the helpful image of a spinning top in her discussion of Kristeva's distinction between Hegel's thetic position and her own in *Reading Kristeva: Unraveling the Double-bind* (Bloomington: Indiana University Press, 1993), 98.

6. See "From Simone DeBeauvoir to Jacques Lacan," in Moi's *Sexual/Textual Politics: Feminist Literary Theory* (New York: Routledge, 2002), 98.

7. See "On *The Samurai*," in *Julia Kristeva Interviews*, ed. Ross M. Guberman (New York: Columbia University Press, 1996), 252.

8. See *Psychoanalytic Politics: Freud's French Revolution* (New York: Basic Books, 1978), 201.

9. See Rose, "Julia Kristeva," 142.

10. I use Symbolist to refer to the French literary movement of the late nineteenth century (*les symbolistes*) and not to Kristeva's concept of symbolic. The latter designates language's denotative and syntactic functions and derives from Saussurian linguistics (see page 14).

11. See Richard Klein, "In the Body of the Mother," *Enclitic* 7, no. 1 (1983): 66–67.

12. DeLaSale is the fifteenth-century novelist discussed in *Desire in Language: A Semiotic Approach to Literature and Art*, trans. Alice Jardine (New York: Columbia University Press, 1980), 36–63; Bakhtin, the Russian critic analyzed in the same volume, 64–91; Guyon, the seventeenth-century mystic writer described in *Tales of Love*, 297–317.

13. Rose discusses the question of origin as problematic in Kristeva in *Sexuality*, 141–60. See also Nancy Fraser's "The Uses and Abuses of French Discourse Theories for Feminist Politics," *boundary 2* 17, no. 2 (1990): 82–101.

14. See Ricoeur's "The Question of Proof in Freud's Psychoanalytic Writings," 198. Ricoeur uses Hegel's distinction between finality and teleology to describe a psychoanalytic teleology in "A Philosophical Interpretation of Freud," *The Philosophy of Paul Ricoeur: An Anthology of His Work* (Boston: Beacon Press, 1978), originally published in 1974, 182.

15. See Lewis's "Revolutionary Semiotics," *Diacritics* 4, no. 3 (1974): 28–32.

16. See Mehlman's *A Structural Study of Autobiography: Proust, Leiris, Sartre, Lévi-Strauss* (Ithaca, NY: Cornell University Press, 1974).

2. A Politics of Desire

This chapter is the revised version of a review essay originally published as "The Politics of Desire in Julia Kristeva," *boundary 2* 12 (1984): 217–28.

1. *Desire in Language: A Semiotic Approach to Literature and Art*, trans. Alice Jardine (New York: Columbia University Press, 1980).

2. Julia Kristeva, *About Chinese Women*, trans. Anita Barrows (London: Marion Boyars, 1977). Kelly Oliver discusses the controversy in *Reading Kristeva*, 134-35.

3. In 1977, Kristeva responded to the charge of elitism in an interview with Jean-Paul Enthoven in "Julia Kristeva: A quoi servent les intellectuels?" *Le Nouvel Observateur*, 20 June 1977, 99.

4. Phillip E. Lewis, "Revolutionary Semiotics," *Diacritics* 4 (Fall 1974): 28-32.

5. Claude Bouché, "Materialist Literary Theory in France, 1965-1975," *Praxis* 5 (1981): 4

6. For a clear example of the American positivist's blindness to Freud, see Adolf Grunbaum, *The Foundations of Psychoanalysis: A Philosophical Critique* (Berkeley and Los Angeles: University of California Press, 1984). Grunbaum, a professor in the philosophy of science, is cited by Frederick Crews, a professor of English, who takes a similar position.

7. Julia Kristeva, "Sujet dans le langage et pratique politique," *Psychanalyse et Politique*, ed. Armando Verdiglione (Paris: Seuil, 1974), 73.

8. See the following works by Bakhtin: *Rabelais and His World*, trans. Helene Iswolsky (Cambridge, MA: MIT Press, 1965); *Problems of Dostoevsky's Poetics*, trans. R. W. Rostel (Ann Arbor, MI: Ardis, 1973); and *The Dialogic Imagination: Four Essays by M. M. Bakhtin*, trans. Caryl Emerson and Michael Holquist, ed. Michael Holquist (Austin: University of Texas Press, 1981).

9. V. N. Volosinov, *Freudianism: A Marxist Critique*, trans. I. R. Titunik (New York: Academic Press, 1976), originally published in 1927.

10. Julia Kristeva, "The Ruin of a Poetics," in *Russian Formalism*, ed. S. Bann and J. Bowit (Edinburgh: Scottish Academic Press, 1973), 109.

11. See my essay "The Text as Dialogue in Bakhtin and Kristeva," *University of Ottawa Quarterly* 53 (1983): 117-24; see also chapter 6 in this volume.

12. See "The Bounded Text," in *Desire in Language*, 51.

13. Ricoeur, "The Question of Proof in Freud's Psychoanalytic Writings," 197-98.

14. See Edmond Wilson, *Axel's Castle: A Study in the Imaginative Literature of 1870-1930* (New York: Scribner's, 1931), 132; and Joseph Frank, *The Widening Gyre: Crisis and Mastery in Modern Literature* (New Brunswick, NJ: Rutgers University Press, 1963), 19-25. See also my "Proust and Psychoanalytic Criticism (PhD diss., State University of New York-Binghamton, 1979), chap. 2.

15. Walter Benjamin, "The Image of Proust," in *Illuminations* (New York: Schocken Books), 206-07.

16. See Serge Doubrovsky, *La Place de la madeleine: Ecriture et fantasme chez Proust* (Paris: Mercure de France, 1974). English translation : *Writing and Fantasy in Proust: La Place de la madeleine*, trans. Carol Mastrangelo Bové with Paul Bové (Lincoln: University of Nebraska Press, 1986).

17. See "Contre l'obscurité," in *Revue blanche*, reprinted in *Contre Sainte Beuve*, ed. Pierre Clarac (Paris: Pléaide, 1971), 390.

18. Marcel Proust, *A La Recherche du temps perdu*, Vols. 1-3 (Paris: Gallimard, 1954). English translation: *Remembrance of Things Past*, 3 vols., trans. C. K. Scott Moncrieff, Terence Kilmartin, and Andreas Mayor (New York: Random House, 1981), 3: 905-6; all references are to this edition.

19. Pierre Zima discusses Proust's social criticism in similar terms but without treating its relationship to narrative point of view and Symbolism. See his *Pour une sociologie du texte littéraire* (Paris: Union générale d'éditions, 1978), 278-88.

20. Leo Bersani reads the episodes of involuntary memory in this way in *A Future for Astyanax: Character and Desire in Literature* (Boston: Little, Brown,1976), 83-85.

21. See Paul DeMan, "Reading (Proust)," in *Allegories of Reading* (New Haven, CT: Yale University Press, 1979), 78.

3. *Psychoanalysis, Feminism, and* Remembrance

Part of this chapter is the revision of an essay originally published as "Women and Society in Literature, or Reading Kristeva and Proust," *Dalhousie Review* (Summer 1984): 260-69.

1. Alice Jardine discusses feminist aspects of Kristeva's theory in "Theories of the Feminine: Kristeva," *Enclitic* 8 (1980): 5-15.

2. For her critique of some feminist theory, see *Tales of Love*, 374.

3. See also Kelly Oliver's analysis of the mother in Kristeva, *Reading Kristeva*, 5-6.

4. I am summarizing Kristeva's reading of Lacan, especially of his notion of the mirror stage. See Jacques Lacan, "Le Stade du miroir comme formateur de la fonction du Je telle qu'elle nous est révélée dans l'expérience psychanalytique," in *Ecrits, I* (Paris: Seuil, 1970), originally published in 1966, 89-97; and Kristeva's *Revolution in Poetic Language* (New York: Columbia University Press), 46-51.

5. Doubrovsky, *La Place de la madeleine*, 14.

6. Ibid., 130.

7. See Bakhtin, *The Dialogic Imagination*, 235-306; Kristeva's commentary on Bakhtin in "Word, Dialogue, and Novel," in *Desire in Language*, 64-91; and my "The Text as Dialogue in Bakhtin and Kristeva," 117-24.

8. See Benjamin's "The Image of Proust," in *Illuminations*, 209.

9. The first two quotations are my translations from Ramon Fernandez, *Proust ou la généologie du roman moderne* (Paris: Grasset, 1979), 184; the following quotations are, respectively, from Harry Levin, *The Gates of Horn: A Study of Five French Realists* (New York: Oxford, 1966), 414; and Bakhtin, *The Dialogic Imagination*, 235-36.

10. Without mentioning its echo in the passage on Saniette, Doubrovsky has focused on the famous madeleine scene as the principal metaphor for unconscious desire in *Remembrance*, see chapter 2 (p. 38) this volume.

11. My translation.

4. Revisiting Modernism

This chapter is a revised version of "Revisiting Modernism with Kristeva: DeBeauvoir, Truffaut, and Renoir," *Journal of Modern Literature* 25, no. 3-4 (Summer 2002): 114-26.

1. See Simone DeBeauvoir, *L'Invitée* (Paris: Gallimard, 1943). English version: *She Came to Stay* (Cleveland, OH: World Publishing, 1954); all page references are to this English translation. *Jules et Jim* [*Jules and Jim*], dir. François Truffaut, 1962; Les Films du Carrosse, 1978; videocassette, CBS/FOX, 1986. *La Règle du jeu* [*Rules of the Game*], dir. Jean Renoir, 1939, videocassette, Kartes.

2. See "Appendix: Sociology, Postmodernity and Exile: An Interview with Zygmunt Bauman, Richard Kilminster and Ian Varcoe," *Intimations of Postmodernity*, Zygmunt Bauman (London: Routledge, 1992), 221.

3. See, for example, *Desire in Language*, 28-32, in which she discusses this male entity in the Russian Futurists; see also chapter 1 (p. 13).

4. Sigmund Freud, *Group Psychology and the Analysis of the Ego*, trans. and ed. James Strachey (New York: Norton, 1959), 33, originally published in German in 1922.

5. See especially Jacques Lacan, "The Function and Field of Speech and Language in Psychoanalysis" and "On a Question Preliminary to any Possible Treatment of Psychosis," in *Ecrits: A Selection*, trans. Alan Sheridan (New York: Norton, 1977), 30-113, 179-225, originally published in French in 1966. See also chapters 1-3 in this volume.

6. "Stabat Mater," in *Tales of Love*, trans. Leon S. Roudiez (New York: Columbia University Press, 1987), 234-63, originally published in French in 1977. See also chapter 1 in this volume.

7. See Jacqueline Rose, "Julia Kristeva—Take Two," in *Ethics, Politics, and Difference in Julia Kristeva's Writing*, ed. Kelly Oliver (New York: Routledge, 1993), 41-61, originally published in 1986.

8. See Paul Ricoeur, "The Question of Proof in Freud's Psychoanalytic Writings," 197-98. See also chapters 1 and 2 in this volume.

9. See *Powers of Horror*, trans. Leon S. Roudiez (New York: Columbia University Press, 1982), originally published in French in 1980; and *Black Sun: Depression and Melancholia*, trans. Leon S. Roudiez (New York: Columbia University Press, 1989), originally published in French in 1987.

10. See Kristeva's *Soleil noir: Dépression et mélancholie* (Paris: Gallimard, 1987), 29.

11. See *Desire in Language*, *Powers of Horror*, and *Time and Sense: Proust and the Experience of Literature*, trans. Ross Guberman (New York: Columbia University Press, 1996). *Time and Sense* was originally published in French in 1994. See also chapters 2 and 3 in this volume.

12. See her "A quoi servent les intellectuels?" *Le Nouvel Observateur*, 29 June 1977, 117.

13. "A New Type of Intellectual: The Dissident," *The Kristeva Reader*, ed. Toril Moi (New York: Columbia University Press, 1986), 296.

14. See Phillip Rieff, *Freud: The Mind of the Moralist* (Chicago: University of Chicago Press, 1959), 162.

15. James Monaco, *The New Wave: Truffaut, Godard, Chabrol, Rohmer, Rivette* (New York: Oxford University Press, 1976), 51.

16. Roger Greenspun, "Elective Affinities: Aspects of *Jules et Jim*," *Sight and Sound* 32, no. 2 (1963): 78.

17. David Davidson, "From Virgin to Dynamo The 'Amoral Woman' in European Cinema," *Cinema Journal* 21, no. 1 (1981): 31–58.

18. Francis Jeanson, *Simone DeBeauvoir ou l'entreprise de vivre* (Paris: Seuil, 1966), 213.

19. Maurice Merleau-Ponty, *Sens et Non-sens* (Paris: Nagel, 1948). English version: *Sense and Non-Sense* (Evanston, IL: Northwestern University Press, 1964), 31–32.

20. Toril Moi, *Simone De Beauvoir: The Making of an Intellectual Woman* (Oxford, UK, Blackwell, 1994), 120.

21. François Truffaut, *Jules et Jim* (1962 ; Paris: Seuil, 1971) English version: *Jules and Jim* (New York: Simon and Schuster, 1968), 11; all page references are to the English edition.

22. See her discussion of maternity in "Women's Time," in *The Kristeva Reader*, 206.

23. See André Bazin, *Jean Renoir*, trans. W. Halsey and W. Simon (New York: Simon and Schuster, 1973), 259.

24. Pierre Leprohon, *Jean Renoir*, trans. B. Elson (New York: Crown, 1971), 167.

25. Judith Maine commented on this upon hearing an earlier version of the essay.

26. Michael Little, "Sound Track: *The Rules of the Game*," *Cinema Journal* 13, no. 1 (1973):35–44.

27. Nick Browne, "Deflections of Desire in *The Rules of the Game*: Reflections on the Theatre of History," *Quarterly Review of Film Studies* 7, no. 3 (1982): 251-61.

28. Julia Lesage, "*S/Z* and *The Rules of the Game*," in *Movies and Methods*, Vol. 2 (Berkeley and Los Angeles: University of California Press, 1985), 476–500.

29. Bazin, *Jean Renoir*, 185.

30. See Robin Bates, "Audiences on the Verge of a Fascist Breakdown: Male Anxieties and Late 1930's French Film," *Cinema Journal* 36, no. 3 (1997): 25–55.

31. *The Dehumanization of Art* (1925; Princeton, NJ: Princeton University Press, 1968), 42.

5. The Two Faces of the Mother's Mask

This chapter is a revised, expanded version of "The Twin Faces of the Mother's Mask: Julia Kristeva's *Powers of Horror: An Essay on Abjection*," *Discourse*, 11, no. 1 (1988-89):151–56.

1. Julia Kristeva, *The Samurai*, trans. Barbara Bray (New York: Columbia University Press, 1994) (*Les samuraïs* [Paris: Fayard, 1990]); *Powers of Horror: An Essay on Abjection*, trans. Leon Roudiez (New York: Columbia University Press, 1982) (*Pouvoirs de l'Horreur* [Paris: Seuil, 1980]); *About Chinese Women*, trans. Anita Barrows (London: Marion Boyars, 1987) (*Des Chinoises*) [Paris: Femmes, 1974]).

2. Louis-Ferdinand Céline, *Voyage au bout de la nuit* (Paris: Denoël et Steele, 1932). English translation: *Journey to the End of the Night*, trans. John H. P. Marks (New York: New Directions, 1934).

3. David O'Connell's analysis of *Journey to the End of the Night* describes how the characters Ferdinand and Léon reveal Céline's ambivalence toward the social. See *Louis-Ferdinand Céline* (Boston: G. K. Hall, Twayne Series, 1976), 51.

4. See Peter Gidal, "On Julia Kristeva," *Undercut: Journal of London Filmmakers Cooperative* 10/11 (1983): 14–19; Jennifer Stone, "The Horrors of Power: A Critique of Kristeva," in *The Politics of Theory*, ed. Barker et al. (Colchester: University of Essex, 1983), 38–48; and Leslie Hill, "Julia Kristeva: Theorizing the Avant-Garde?" in *Abjection, Melancholia and Love* (London: Routledge, 1990), 137–56. Hill also supplies the autobiographical information on Céline's mother discussed earlier.

5. See, for instance, Moi's discussion of those critics who see Kristeva as an essentialist in *Sexual/Textual Politics*.

6. See Cynthia Chase, "L'Objet d'amour, *Tel Quel* 91,": *Criticism* 26, no. 2 (1984): 195.

7. Gayatri Spivak, "French Feminism in an International Frame," in *In Other Worlds: Essays in Cultural Politics* (New York: Methuen, 1987), 134–53. Page numbers refer to this chapter.

8. *About Chinese Women*, p. 7, note.

9. Spivak, "French Feminism in an International Frame," 140.

10. See also Arif Dirlik, who gives evidence of a possible matriarchal history though he does not explicitly discuss it, in *Revolution and History: Origins of Marxist Historiography in China, 1919–1937* (Berkeley and Los Angeles: University of California Press, 1978), 144, 155–56, 173–75.

11. Josyane Leclerc Riboni shows the ways in which Kristeva rejects existential engagement and an orthodox Marxist orientation in *The Samurai* and puts forward a psychoanalytic theory and practice. Riboni's suggestion that the novel celebrates the "free world," especially the United States, is not convincing given Kristeva's satire of American consumer society in this novel. See *Des Mandarins aux Samouraïs: La Fin d'un mythe* (New York: Peter Lang, 1997).

12. See *Revolution in Poetic Language*, trans. Margaret Waller (New York: Columbia University Press, 1984), a translation of *La Révolution du langage poétique* (Paris: Editions du Seuil, 1974);

Black Sun, trans. Leon S. Roudiez (New York: Columbia Univesity Press, 1989), a translation of *Soleil Noir: Dépression et mélancolie* (Paris: Editions Gallimard, 1987); *The Old Man and the Wolves*, trans. Barbara Bray (New York: Columbia University Press, 1994), a translation of *Le vieil homme et les loups* (Paris: Fayard, 1991); and *Possessions*, trans. Barbara Bray (New York: Columbia University Press, 1998), a translation of *Possessions* (Paris: Fayard, 1996). All page references are to the translations.

13. "Take Two," in *Sexuality in the Field of Vision* (London: New Left Books, 1986), 162.

6. Kristeva's Work in the Eighties

1. See *Tales of Love*, trans. Leon S. Roudiez (New York: Columbia University Press, 1987), originally published as *Histoires d'amour* (Paris: Seuil, 1984); *In the Beginning Was Love: Psychoanalysis and Faith*, trans. Arthur Goldhammer (New York: Columbia University Press, 1987), originally published as *Au Commencement était l'amour: Psychanalyse et foi* (Paris: Hachette, 1985); and *Black Sun: Depression and Melancholia*, trans. Léon S. Roudiez (New York: Columbia University Press, 1989), originally published as *Soleil noir: Dépression et mélancholie* (Paris: Gallimard, 1987).

2. See, for instance, a recent review of *Tales of Love* and *In the Beginning Was Love* by Leslie Rabine in *L'Esprit Créateur* 29, no. 1 (1989): 100–101; and Toril Moi's critique of such charges in *Textual/Sexual Politics*, 165–66.

3. See Leslie Hill's "Julia Kristeva," 154.

4. See Jeffrey Kripal's *Roads of Excess, Palaces of Wisdom: Eroticism and Reflexivity in the Study of Mysticism* (Chicago: University of Chicago Press, 2004).

5. See Jacqueline Rose's "Julia Kristeva—Take Two." See also Toril Moi's reading of Kristeva within the framework of feminist literary theory in "Marginality and Subversion: Julia Kristeva," in *Textual/Sexual Politics*, 150–73.

7. Fiction, Fact, and Theory

1. Julia Kristeva, *The Old Man and the Wolves*, trans. Barbara Bray (New York: Columbia University Press, 1994) (*Le vieil homme et les loups* [Paris: Fayard, 1991]); *Possessions*, trans. Barbara Bray (New York: Columbia University Press, 1998) (*Possessions* [Paris: Fayard, 1996]); *Feminine Genius: Life, Madness, Words–Hannah Arendt, Melanie Klein, and Colette* (1999–2002) (*Le Génie féminin: La vie, la folie, les mots: Hannah Arendt, Melanie Klein, Colette*, 3 vols. [Paris: Fayard, 2002]); and *The Samurais*, trans. Barbara Bray (New York: Columbia University Press, 1994) (*Les Samuraïs* [Paris: Fayard, 1990]).

2. See the interview in *L'Infini* 79 (Summer 2002): 76.

3. See Sigmund Freud, *Group Psychology and the Analysis of the Ego*, trans. and ed. James Strachey (New York: Norton, 1959), 33, originally published in German in 1922.

4. See "Julia Kristeva and Her Old Man: Between Optimism and Despair," *Textual Practice* 7, no. 1 (Spring 1993): 1–12.

5. See Michael Wood "Time of the Assassin," *London Review of Books*, 26 Jan. 1995, 18.

6. See *Julia Kristeva Interviews*, ed. Ross M. Guberman (New York: Columbia University Press, 1996), 169.

7. See *Le Génie féminin: La vie, la folie, les mots: Hannah Arendt, Melanie Klein, Colette*, 3 vols. (Paris: Fayard, 2002).

8. *Hannah Arendt*, trans. Ross Guberman (New York: Columbia University Press, 2001) (*Le Génie Féminin, Hannah Arendt* [Paris: Fayard, 1999]).

9. *Melanie Klein*, trans. Ross Guberman (New York: Columbia University Press, 2001) (*Le Génie féminin, Melanie Klein* [Paris: Fayard, 2000]).

10. *L'Enfant et les Sortilèges* (Paris: A. Durand et fils, 1925).

11. *Les Vrilles de la vigne*, in *Oeuvres*, vol. 1 (Paris: Gallimard, 1984), originally published in 1908.

12. "Female Sexuality," in *The Standard Edition of the Complete Psychological Works of Sigmund Freud*, vol. 21 (London: Hogarth, 1953–73), originally published in 1931, 223–43.

13. *My Mother's House*, trans. U. V. Troubridge and E. McLeod (Westport, CT: Greenwood Press, 1953) (*La Maison de Claudine*, in *Oeuvres*, vol. 2 [Paris: Gallimard, 1986]), originally published in 1922. Page references are to the English translation.

14. Jerry A. Flieger writes at length on the theme of circularity in Colette and her use of a circular or vertical rather than linear structure in her texts. See *Colette and the Fantom Subject of Autobiography* (Ithaca, NY: Cornell University Press, 1992), 35–43, 187.

15. Virginia Best, *Critical Subjectivities: Identity and Narrative in the Works of Colette and Marguerite Duras* (Geneva: Peter Lang, 2000), 131–32.

16. Kaja Silverman, *The Acoustic Mirror: The Female Voice in Psychoanalysis and Cinema* (Bloomington: Indiana University Press, 1988), 102.

17. See *Colette*, 438; and Judith Thurmon's *Secrets of the Flesh: A Life of Colette* (New York: Knopf, 1999), 474.

18. Diana Fuss, *Identification Papers* (New York: Routledge, 1995).

Conclusion

1. See Fuss's *Identification Papers*, O'Hara's articles in *Journal of Modern Literature* 25, no. 3–4 (Summer 2002); and Irigaray's *Sexes and Genealogies*, trans. Gillian Gill (New York: Columbia University Press, 1993), originally published as *Sexes et Parentés*, 1987.

2. See Fuss, Introduction.

3. See *Sexes and Genealogies*, 5.

4. See *Sexuality in the Field of Vision*, 141–64.

5. See Paul Ricoeur, "The Question of Proof in Freud's Psychoanalytic Writings," in *The Philosophy of Paul Ricoeur: An Anthology of His Works* (Boston: Beacon Press, 1978), originally published in 1977, 197–98.

6. See, for example, Jennifer Stone, "The Horrors of Power: A Critique of Kristeva," in *The Politics of Theory: Proceedings of the Essex Conference on the Sociology of Literature, July 1982*, ed. Barker, Francis et al. (Colchester: University of Essex, 1983), 38–48.

7. See *Julia Kristeva Interviews*.

8. See Best, 131–132.

9. *Colette*, 474.

✿ Index ✿

abjection, 6, 65–66, 81, 83–86, 91
androgyny, 90, 99, 123, 148
anti-Semitism, 87, 90

Bakhtin, Mikhail, 4, 6, 19, 27, 29,
 31, 32–35, 39, 42, 50–51, 58, 106,
 115, 135, 149–50. *See also* Volosinov, V. N.
Barthes, Roland, 4, 27, 77, 98
Beauvoir, Simone De, 3, 15, 16, 45,
 145, 149, 151; *She Came to Stay*,
 15, 63–64, 67–74, 76, 81, 151
Bible, 9, 86, 107–8; *Song of Songs*,
 107–8, 110, 134

Céline, Louis-Ferdinand, 4, 6, 27, 65,
 66, 83, 143, 151–52; *Voyage to the
 End of the Night*, 9, 84, 86–90
Cixous, Hélène, 1, 2, 18, 46, 138;
 Exile of James Joyce, 13
Clairvaux, Bernard De, 107–8, 153
Colette, 134, 136–46, 154–55

DeLaSale, Antoine, 4, 9, 19, 27–28,
 35–36, 135, 150

Essentialism, 2, 6, 12, 19–23, 151, 154
Existentialism, 67–68; Marxist, 15

feminism, 5, 20, 45–43, 61. 83, 94,
 118, 143
Freud, Sigmund, 2–4, 12–13, 16–17,
 21, 34, 45, 48, 63–€5, 66, 69, 74,
 84–85, 91, 95, 102, 106–8, 109,
 112, 115, 122–23, 132, 135,
 145–151; *Group Psychology*, 7;
 "Psychogenesis of a Case of
 Homosexuality in a Woman," 145;
 Ricoeur and, 13
Fuss, Diana, 145, 147. 154

Guyon, Jeanne, 7, 19, 109

Hegel, 12–17, 22, 30; "thetic position"
 and, 4, 13, 18, 20

Irigaray, Luce, 1, 2, 45, 147–48

Kristeva, Julia: *About Chinese Women*,
 3–4, 6, 28, 45–46, 83–84, 90,
 92–97, 100, 102–3, 150, 152;
 Black Sun, 7, 17, 20 90, 102,
 105–6, 111, 114, 117–19, 121,
 153; *Colette*, 4, 6, 8, 11, 106, 121,
 134–36, 138–39, 143–46, 154,
 155; *Desire in Language*, 4, 27–37,
 45, 123, 149–50; *Feminine Genius*, 6,

171